# *Stand Fast in Liberty*

## An Exposition of Galatians

Robert G. Gromacki

**Baker Book House**
**Grand Rapids, Michigan**

To
my brother
RON
and
his family

# *Contents*

# *Preface*

It is fashionable today to be born again, but many who make this profession are not really saved. They are not really justified by faith alone; they believe that they still must do something to contribute to their own salvation. In the first century many added circumcision and obedience to the Mosaic law to faith in Christ as conditions for entrance into heaven. In this day there have been other substitutions (e.g. baptism, confirmation), but the principle has remained the same: they are trying to be saved by faith *and* works.

Paul attacked this doctrine tenaciously. Legalism can never provide justification or sanctification. The principles of grace must always govern salvation and service.

In our day the Book of Galatians is extremely relevant. Just as Martin Luther discovered its truth, so it must be rediscovered by the evangelical world. Legalism has again crept into the messages of the churches, and therefore the churches must be alerted once more.

This study has been designed to teach the Word of God to others. It is an attempt to make clear the meaning of the English text (King James Version) through organization, exposition, and careful usage of the Greek text. It is planned as a readable study through a nontechnical vocabulary and smooth transition from one section to another.

Divided into thirteen chapters, it can be used by adult Sunday school classes or Bible study groups for a typical quarter of thirteen weeks. Also it can be adapted easily into a six-month study by devoting two sessions to each chapter. Concluding each chapter are discussion questions, designed to stimulate personal inquiry and to make the truth of God relevant. In addition, this book can be used by one person as a private Bible study guide. In either case, this exposition should be read with an open Bible. The actual English text is indicated throughout by use of quotation marks. It is the author's prayer that men and women will be blessed and edified as they undertake this study of Galatians.

A special word of thanks is extended to Cornelius Zylstra, editor of Baker Book House, who encouraged me to write this exposition. Also my love and appreciation go to my wife, Gloria, who carefully typed the manuscript.

# *Introduction*

Galatians has been called both the Magna Charta of Christian Liberty and the Christian Declaration of Independence. Out of its pages grew the Protestant Reformation, for it was by study in Galatians that Luther's heart was opened to the truth of justification by faith alone.

## I. WRITER

Even critical liberals acknowledge the Pauline authorship of this book. There is nothing within the book or the writings of the church fathers that would cause anyone to question its authenticity. The author called himself Paul twice (1:1; 5:2). The many historical references can be harmonized with the events of Acts and of the other Epistles: his pharisaical Jewish heritage (1:13–14; cf. Acts 22:3), his persecution of the church (1:13; cf. Acts 7:58; 8:1–3), his dramatic conversion on the way to Damascus (1:15–17; cf. Acts 9:1–25), his visit to Jerusalem (1:18; cf. Acts 11:30), his home church at Antioch (2:11; cf. Acts 13:1), his physical problems (4:15; 6:11; cf. II Cor. 12:7–10), and his persecutions (6:12, 17; cf. II Cor. 11:23–27).

## II. REGION OF GALATIA

About the fourth century B.C., barbarians migrated from north of the Black Sea westward into Macedonia, Greece, and

France. Some tribes broke away and moved into north-central Asia Minor. Here they were called *Galatai* by the Greeks and *Galla* by the Romans; thus the territory came to be known as *Galatia*. The Romans looked on the Galatians as allies, but when their leader Amyntas died, their region was annexed as a Roman province by Caesar Augustus in 25 B.C. He enlarged the province by adding part of Pontus to the northeast, part of Phrygia to the southwest, and most of Lycaonia to the south. The geographical limits were constantly changing, but in the New Testament era it was a large province bordered by other such provinces as Asia (west), Cappadocia (east), Pamphylia and Cilicia (south), and Bithynia and Pontus (north). The southern and southwestern sections of the province were more densely populated because here the cities were connected by a network of Roman roads; thus southern Galatia became more important politically and economically. Within this region were the cities evangelized by Paul and Barnabas during their first missionary journey: Antioch in Pisidia, Iconium, Lystra, and Derbe.

The Galatians had adopted the mythological polytheism of the Greeks and the Romans. Just as the Cretans were known for their lying (Titus 1:12), so the Galatians were known nationally as an impulsive, fickle, and inconsistent people. This could be seen in their paradoxical desire to worship Paul at one moment and to stone him the next (Acts 14:11–19) and also in their quickness to receive the gospel and to abandon it (1:6).

## III. ESTABLISHMENT OF THE CHURCHES

Paul and Barnabas evangelized the southern section of the Roman province of Galatia during Paul's first missionary journey (Acts 13:14—14:26). After reaching the mainland from Cyprus they moved quickly from Perga in Pamphylia to Antioch in Pisidia, a mountainous region which provided a refuge for thieves and Roman political enemies (cf. II Cor. 11:26). Antioch, a city founded by Seleucus I Nicator (312-280 B.C.), was a center of commerce on the trade route between Ephesus

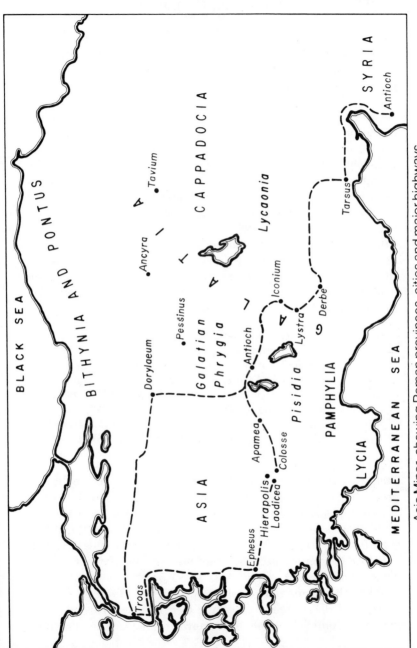

Asia Minor, showing Roman provinces, cities and major highways.

to the west and the Cilician Gates to the east. On the Sabbath they went into the synagogue where Paul was given the opportunity to preach to the congregation of Jews and Gentile proselytes (Acts 13:16, 26). In his sermon he identified the messianic hope of the Old Testament with Jesus Christ in His death and resurrection and proclaimed that forgiveness of sins and justification could be received only through faith in Him, not through legal obedience (Acts 13:38–39). After the Jews, apparently offended at his message, stormed out of the synagogue, the Gentiles present extended an invitation to Paul to preach the same sermon on the next Sabbath (Acts 13:42). As the result of this first proclamation, many Jews and Gentiles ("religious proselytes") were converted (Acts 13:43). When "almost the whole city" showed up at the synagogue to hear Paul the next Sabbath, the Jews were filled with jealousy because Paul had reached more Gentiles in one week than they had in several years of endeavor. When they attacked Paul he countered with a stirring ultimatum:

> ... It was necessary that the word of God should first have been spoken to you: but seeing ye put it from you, and judge yourselves unworthy of everlasting life, lo, we turn to the Gentiles. For so hath the Lord commanded us, saying, I have set thee to be a light of the Gentiles, that thou shouldest be for salvation unto the ends of the earth. And when the Gentiles heard this, they were glad, and glorified the word of the Lord: and as many as were ordained to eternal life believed (Acts 13:46–48).

From this point on in his ministry Paul followed the policy of preaching to the Jews first and then to the Gentiles after Jewish opposition began. The ministry among the Gentiles met with great success (Acts 13:49, 52), but Paul and Barnabas were forced to leave when "the Jews stirred up the devout and honourable women, and the chief men of the city, and raised persecution against" them (Acts 13:50–51).

When they came to Iconium they preached in the synagogue there; as a result, many Jews and Gentile proselytes believed in Christ. Again the unbelieving Jews influenced the unbelieving Gentiles against the converts. In spite of this opposition, Paul and Barnabas stayed "a long time," preaching and performing miracles. Although the city was divided over their ministry, the unbelieving Jews and Gentiles plus their rulers determined to kill the apostles. When the latter learned of the plot they fled to Lystra and Derbe (Acts 14:1–6).

These two cities were located in Lycaonia, a small landlocked province noted for its flat pasture land. The people there spoke a language composed of corrupt Greek mixed with Assyrian. Lystra was about eighteen miles southwest of Iconium; Derbe, a small town at the base of Mount Taurus, was sixteen miles east of Lystra.

At Lystra Paul healed a lame man, crippled through birth defects. When the pagans witnessed the miracle they thought that the apostles were gods in the likeness of men (Barnabas as Jupiter and Paul as Mercury) and planned to offer animal sacrifices to them. Barnabas and Paul restrained the people from doing so through a brief sermon in which Paul admonished them to turn from their paganism to the living God of creation. Shortly after, Jews from Antioch and Iconium came to Lystra, stoned Paul, and dragged him out of the city. Paul, however, revived and went on to Derbe (Acts 14:6–20).

After preaching in Derbe, Paul and Barnabas retraced their steps through Lystra, Iconium, and Antioch teaching, comforting, and appointing leaders in the churches they had just started (Acts 14:21–23). They ended their journey by returning to Antioch (Acts 14:24–26).

## IV. DESTINATION OF THE LETTER

To what churches of Galatia (1:2; 3:1) did Paul write? This moot question has bothered commentators for generations. Although the answer does not affect the message of the book, it does determine the time of its composition. *Two major views* have been proposed. The *first* is that Paul wrote to churches within the old territory of north Galatia, a region that he evangelized during his second journey and revisited during his third (Acts 16:6; 18:23). The proponents argue that Luke used territorial, not Roman provincial, titles to describe the regions encompassed by Paul's itinerary (Acts 13:14; 14:6; 16:6; 18:23). However, it is difficult to determine the real meaning of Luke's words. Literally he said that Paul went through "the Phrygian-Galatic country" (Acts 16:6) and later through "the Galatic-Phrygian country" (Acts 18:23). This is a general designation and could refer to either the territory or province or both. The advocates add that since there is no mention of Paul's physical infirmity during the first journey (Acts 13-14), why would Paul refer to it in the letter (4:13)? However, Luke does not mention it in his accounts of the second or third journeys either. Many of Paul's persecutions and illnesses were not recorded by Luke or even by Paul himself (cf. II Cor. 11-12). They further suggest that Paul would have referred to his persecutions, including the stoning episode, if he had written to the south Galatian churches. But Paul did mention the marks (stigmata) that his body bore for his faith and testimony (6:17); also it is conceivable that his eye problem (4:13-15) was caused or aggravated by the stoning incident.

In positive support for the *second* view that Paul wrote to those churches founded on the first journey, many have pointed out that Acts contains territorial designations whereas Paul chose to use provincial titles. In I Corinthians Paul alluded to the churches of Galatia (16:1); in that same context he referred to other regions by their provincial names: Macedonia (16:5), Achaia (16:15), and Asia (16:19). Thus he most likely used *Galatia* as a provincial title. It is also more likely that Paul wrote to churches whose establishment is recorded in Acts (chs. 13-14) than to churches about which we have little information. Judaizers, the enemies of Paul, would have invaded the densely populated areas of southern Galatia where Jews and synagogues were located rather than the sparsely settled northern sections. The reference to Barnabas, especially his defection at Antioch (2:1, 9; cf. 2:13), would only have significance to the southern Galatians, because Barnabas was with Paul during the first journey but not during the next two. Since there is no reference to the historic decision made at the council of Jerusalem (Acts 15), a decision that would have provided

Paul with a clinching argument, the book must have been written before that event occurred. In that case, Paul could only have written to the south Galatian churches of Antioch, Iconium, Lystra, and Derbe. Although Peter was an unstable person at times, his defection at Antioch (2:11–14) would better fit into his life experiences before the council at Jerusalem than after.

Finally, the several biographical references in the first two chapters correlate better with a south Galatian destination. The visit to Jerusalem in which he saw Peter and James (1:18–19; cf. Acts 9:26) occurred three years after his conversion (A.D. 32; cf. A.D. 35). The second visit to Jerusalem, which happened fourteen years after his conversion rather than after his first visit, probably was the famine visit rather than the trip to attend the council meeting (2:1; cf. Acts 11:29, 30; A.D. 46). The council was a public, general meeting (Acts 15), whereas the visit of Paul, Barnabas, and Titus was private (2:2). The recognition of Paul's apostleship and message by the Jerusalem apostles certainly would have taken place before the council meeting. In the intervening years between the two Jerusalem visits, Paul spent nine in Tarsus (A.D. 35-44) and labored for two more in Syrian Antioch (A.D. 44-46).

## V. TIME AND PLACE

Most of the older commentators favored the north Galatian theory. If they were correct, the epistle had to be written during Paul's third journey, probably from either Ephesus or Macedonia (A.D. 53-56).

Contemporary scholarship has embraced the south Galatian view. This would mean that the letter could have been written at any time after the completion of the first journey (A.D. 47-48). It has been dated from Corinth during the second journey (Zahn; A.D. 50-52), from Antioch just before the beginning of the third journey (Ramsey; A.D. 52), and from Macedonia or Greece during the third journey (Thiessen; A.D. 55-56). Most modern advocates of this theory place the writing of Galatians in Antioch just before the Jerusalem council (Gromacki, Tenney; A.D. 48–49). Consequently, after Paul and Barnabas returned to Antioch after their first journey, Peter visited them and the church at Antioch. There he fellowshipped with the Gentile Christians, withdrew from them, and was reproved publicly by Paul. Judaizers meanwhile had invaded the south Galatian churches, teaching the necessity of circumcision to gain and to maintain salvation and denying Paul's apostleship. When Paul received the report of this theological dilemma he wrote Galatians prior to his attendance at the Jerusalem council.

## VI. PURPOSES

The purposes naturally grew out of the theological predicament of the churches. In the first two chapters Paul attempted to vindicate his apostleship and message which were under attack through answers to these questions: where did he get his apostolic authority and message, and who accepted him as an apostle? Through constant autobiographical references he demonstrated that his apostolic office was given directly by Christ and that it was recognized by the Jerusalem apostles. In so doing he made Galatians the second most autobiographical of his epistles, next to II Corinthians.

In the next two chapters (3–4) he logically explained and defended the doctrine of justification by faith. It was basically a counterattack against the false teaching that circumcision and legal obedience were necessary in addition to faith to secure a complete salvation.

The final two chapters (5–6) contain instructions for practical Christian living. The early section describes the Spirit-controlled life (5:1—6:10), whereas the closing paragraphs deal with warnings against the Judaizers (6:11–18).

The Judaizers were probably Judean Jews who penetrated the recently established Gentile churches of Galatia, warning them: "Except ye be circumcised after the manner of Moses, ye cannot be saved" (cf. Acts 15:1). They regarded the Gentile believers as second-class spiritual citizens who needed to become Jewish in their approach to God. This proclamation would have appealed to the unsaved Galatian Jews who resisted and persecuted Paul (Acts 13:41, 45, 50–51; 14:1–5, 19). It is possible that these Judaizers accused Paul of preaching the necessity of circumcision to Jewish audiences, but not to Gentile crowds (cf. 5:11); thus they were saying that Paul was a coward and a spiritual compromiser. It is conceivable that some of the Galatians had succumbed to the influence of the Judaizers and that the former were even trying to convert their friends (6:13). To Paul the situation was desperate. This is probably why his typical salutation of grace and peace did not include a prayer of thanksgiving for them. To impress the readers with his own urgent concern, Paul either wrote the entire letter himself or at least the closing section (6:11–18). In either case, he did not use an amanuensis or secretary in his normal fashion. The Galatians would have been emotionally moved when they saw the large letters of the Pauline script (6:11).[1] The severe spiritual tone of the letter can also be seen in Paul's condemnation of the false teachers (1:7, 9; 5:10, 12; 6:17).

It should also be observed that this is the only epistle to be written by Paul to a group of churches. All others were sent to either individual churches or persons.

---

[1]Literally: "Behold what large letters I have written to you by my own hand." The KJV "how large a letter" is misleading. The book was not lengthy, but the size of the Greek print was exceptionally large, due to Paul's poor eyesight (cf. 4:15).

# 1

## The Curse on a False Gospel
### Galatians 1:1–9

The apostle was under attack by his religious enemies and under suspicion by his supposed friends. The Judaizers, who taught that a sinner was justified by God through faith in Christ plus obedience to the Mosaic law, claimed that Paul was not a genuine apostle and that his message omitted the necessity of circumcision and legalism as an accommodation to a pagan Gentile culture. Paul was accustomed to such false charges. What disturbed him greatly was that the very churches which he had founded on his first missionary journey were questioning his apostolic credentials. In fact, these Pauline converts began to wonder whether the apostle had communicated only partial truth to them.

These slanderous attacks had to be repelled. To Paul the authenticity of his apostleship and the integrity of his message were inseparably joined. He had to defend both in order to rescue the churches and to turn back his critics.

Thus an atmosphere of seriousness pervades not only his opening remarks but the entire epistle. To Paul a holy war was now in progress. Immediately he staged a counteroffensive. Unlike his other epistles, the apostle did not begin with a prayer of thanksgiving for his converts (cf. Rom. 1:8; I Cor. 1:4; Eph. 1:15–16; Phil. 1:3; Col. 1:3; I Thess. 1:2). Even though these other churches had moral and doctrinal problems, Paul could still thank God for them. However, he could not do this for the Galatian churches.

## I. BASIS OF THE TRUE GOSPEL (1:1-5)

Prior to His ascension into heaven, Jesus Christ commissioned the apostles: "Go ye into all the world, and preach the gospel to every creature" (Mark 16:15; cf. Matt. 28:18-20; Luke 24:46-47). Authorized men were sent to proclaim an authorized message. But what is the gospel? And who are real apostles?

### A. Genuine Messenger (1:1-3)

Since Paul was not one of the original twelve apostles (cf. Matt. 10:1-4), he had to demonstrate that his apostleship was the same as theirs. He claimed neither superiority nor inferiority; rather he asserted an equality.

#### 1. His Name (1:1a)

In his pre-Christian life Paul was known as Saul of Tarsus, the persecutor of the church (Acts 7:58; 8:1, 3; 9:1). When Christ revealed Himself to the young Pharisee He addressed the latter as Saul (Acts 9:4). For the next nine years of his Christian life he maintained the usage of his given name (Acts 9:17, 19, 22, 26; 11:25, 30; 13:1-2).

At the beginning of his first missionary journey, however, he changed his name to Paul (cf. Acts 13:9, 13). On this occasion, at Cyprus, Paul demonstrated his apostolic authority for the first time by imposing blindness on the sorcerer Elymas who had resisted the gospel witness. Through this miracle Paul won his first convert, the Roman proconsul Sergius Paulus (Acts 13:7-12). It is plausible that Saul assumed the name of Paul (*Paulos*) as a constant reminder of the grace and power of God who can save sinners and call them to Christian service.[1]

The Latin *paulus* means "little" or "small." Before a mighty God, Paul saw himself in this humble fashion: "Unto me, who am less than the least of all saints, is this grace given, that I should preach among the Gentiles the unsearchable riches of

[1]Two early church fathers, Jerome and Augustine, both believed that Paul took his new name from Sergius Paulus.

Christ" (Eph. 3:8). Late in life, the apostle still viewed himself as the "chief" of sinners (I Tim. 1:15).

Born into the Jewish tribe of Benjamin, he was probably named by his parents after the name of the first king of Israel (Phil. 3:5; cf. I Sam. 9:1–2). King Saul, who was tall physically, was humbled by God because of his pride and arrogant self-will. The proud Pharisee was also humbled by God on the road to Damascus, but he arose to become a dedicated servant of Christ.

Thus his very name manifested the spiritual transformation in his life accomplished by the divine gospel of saving grace.

### 2. His Position (1:1b)

Throughout the centuries of biblical history, the authority of God's official spokesmen has been questioned. The exclusive leadership of Moses was doubted even by Miriam and Aaron, his own sister and brother (Num. 12:1, 2). The priests and Levites rejected the credentials of John the Baptist (John 1:19–25). Even Jesus Christ was asked by His religious critics: "By what authority doest thou these things? and who gave thee this authority?" (Matt. 21:23). In all of these situations men clearly rejected the divine authentication of these prophets and thus refused to obey their prophetic messages.

In the face of religious hostility Paul made four claims about his official position. *First,* he strongly asserted that he was "an apostle." Apostles were those believers who had seen the resurrected Christ and who had been commanded directly by Him to preach and to lay the foundation for the church age (Eph. 2:20). Their ministries were marked by miraculous authentication and by the obedience of genuine, spiritual Christians (Mark 16:17, 20; Heb. 2:3–4). Few men qualified for this apostolic position: the twelve, Matthias (Acts 1:26), Barnabas (Acts 14:4, 14), James (Gal. 1:19), and Paul. The sound of apostolic authority rings throughout his epistles (Rom. 15:18–19; I Cor. 4:18–21; Phil. 4:9; Col. 1:25; 4:16, 17; I Thess. 5:27). He claimed the official title for himself several times (Rom. 1:1; I Cor. 1:1; II Cor. 1:1; Eph. 1:1; Col. 1:1; I Tim. 1:1; II Tim. 1:1; Titus 1:1). To the Corinthians and to all churches he could honestly say:

"Truly the signs of an apostle were wrought among you in all patience, in signs, and wonders, and mighty deeds" (II Cor. 12:12). He debated with logical, rhetorical questions: "Am I not an apostle? am I not free? have I not seen Jesus Christ our Lord? are not ye my work in the Lord?" (I Cor. 9:1). There can be no doubt that Paul claimed to be an apostle. However, he knew that a claim *per se* does not demonstrate its own truthfulness. He had to prove his assertion; then the Galatians had to decide whether Paul's defense of his apostleship was true or false.

*Second,* he denied that his apostleship originated with men ("not of men"). Literally it reads "not from (*apo*) men." Paul, along with others, was a prophetic teacher who ministered within the church at Syrian Antioch (Acts 13:1). At that time he received his missionary call:

> As they ministered to the Lord, and fasted, the Holy Ghost said, Separate me Barnabas and Saul for the work whereunto I have called them. And when they had fasted and prayed, and laid their hands on them, they sent them away (Acts 13:2–3).

The verb "sent" (*apelusan*) is not the same as the one used for an apostolic commission (*apostellō*).[2] The associates at Antioch did not appoint Paul or Barnabas to the position of apostle; they simply recognized the divine selection of the two.

In the interval between the ascension of Christ into heaven and the descent of the Holy Spirit on the day of Pentecost, the eleven apostles selected Matthias over Joseph Barsabas to be the apostolic replacement for Judas Iscariot (Acts 1:21–26). The choice was made through prayer and the casting of lots. However, there is no indication that God authorized this

---

[2]The Greek word *apostolos,* translated "apostle," comes from the verb *apostellō,* which means to send away with a commission to do something. The original twelve apostles were selected from among many disciples to be with Christ and to be sent forth by Him to preach, heal, and cast out demons within Israel (Matt. 10:5–8; Mark 3:13–15). Excluding Judas Iscariot, this group was later recommissioned by the resurrected Christ to preach the gospel throughout the world (Matt. 28:16–20).

means of appointment. In a real sense, it could be said that Matthias was an apostle "of men."

Others could have suggested that the apostles at Jerusalem, especially Peter, James, and John, officially conferred on Paul their title when he visited the holy city fourteen years after his conversion (Gal. 2:1–10). Paul explained, however, that these apostles simply recognized that God had also called the former Pharisee to the apostleship years before he met the original twelve.

*Third,* he also denied the allegation that one man had appointed him to the office ("neither by man"). The significant change from the plural ("men") to the singular ("man") must be observed. The Judaizers could have easily charged that Paul was indebted to Ananias for the former's conversion and call into the ministry (Acts 9:10–17). After all, the regenerated Saul received his sight and was filled with the Holy Spirit when Ananias laid his hands upon the apostle (Acts 9:17). However, Ananias was informed by Christ that Paul was chosen to be an apostle by Him before His appearance to Ananias and before Ananias contacted Paul.

These critics could have also suggested that Barnabas was humanly responsible for Paul's ministry. It is true that Barnabas introduced Paul to the apostles at Jerusalem (Acts 9:27), that Barnabas brought Paul to work in the church at Antioch (Acts 11:25–26), and that the name of Barnabas regularly appeared before that of Paul (Acts 11:30; 12:25; 13:1, 2, 7; 14:12, 14). Yet the Bible nowhere implies that Barnabas made Paul into an apostle. This same critical argument of debt through association could also be ridiculously applied to the apostleship of Peter who actually was introduced by his brother Andrew to Christ (John 1:40–42).

*Fourth,* he boldly stated that his apostleship had divine origin.[3] Both God the Son and God the Father were the heavenly source of his authority.[4] Christ saved Paul through His ap-

---

[3]The strong adversative "but" (*alla*) marks an abrupt distinction between the negative and the positive sources of his position.

[4]The two Persons serve as the double object of the single preposition "by" (*dia*).

pearance to him on the road to Damascus (Acts 9:3–6). On that occasion the Savior said, "But rise, and stand upon thy feet: for I have appeared unto thee for this purpose, to make thee a minister and a witness both of these things which thou hast seen, and of those things in the which I will appear unto thee" (Acts 26:16). Paul knew that he had seen the resurrected Christ and that he had been directly commissioned by Him (I Cor. 9:1; 15:8–10).

He was a called apostle of Jesus Christ "through the will of God" (I Cor. 1:1). Later Paul wrote that "it pleased God, who separated me from my mother's womb, and called me by his grace, to reveal his Son in me" (Gal. 1:15–16). The Father and the Son always work in concert. The Father is further described as the one "who raised him [Jesus] from the dead." The original twelve became apostles during Christ's earthly ministry and were later recommissioned after His resurrection (Matt. 10:1–4; 28:18–20). However, Paul did not know Christ during His earthly life. He was called to be an apostle by the Savior after His death and resurrection.

### 3. His Associates (1:2a)

Instead of naming his companions individually, Paul identified those who supported him as "all the brethren which are with me." If Paul did write this letter from Antioch in the interval between his first and second missionary journeys, the "brethren" would refer to the believers in the apostle's home church, to Barnabas, and to the prophets and teachers with whom he had ministered earlier (Acts 13:1). The believers at Antioch were the first to be given the name *Christians* (Acts 11:26). Paul used the word *brethren* for both his associates and his readers (4:12; 5:11; 6:1). This served to join the two groups into a single unit, a body of sinners redeemed by divine grace and born into the family of God through faith in the crucified, resurrected Christ.

### 4. His Readers (1:2b)

This is the only letter written by the apostle to a group of churches. His other epistles were addressed to either single churches or to individuals. The "churches of Galatia" refer to those assemblies of believers started during the first missionary journey by Paul and Barnabas (Acts 13:1—14:28). They were located in the cities of Pisidian Antioch, Iconium, Lystra, and Derbe. They consisted of believers who had been baptized, who had united with each other for mutual fellowship, instruction, and evangelization, and who were under the leadership of appointed pastor-elders (Acts 14:22-23). Although these churches were autonomous units, they were, in a way, interdependent. Believers need spiritual strength from other Christians within a local church, but churches controlled by scriptural principles will also sense a need of cooperation with other churches.

### 5. His Blessing (1:3)

The content of the blessing was twofold: "grace" and "peace." These two words reflect both Greek ("grace," *charis*) and Hebrew ("peace," *shalom*) concepts. Grace precedes and is always the basis for peace. The doctrine of grace reveals that God bestows blessings upon believers apart from any merit within them. Grace has been defined as "*G*od's *R*iches *A*t *C*hrist's *E*xpense." When repentant sinners are justified by the grace of God, they enjoy a position of peace before God (Rom. 3:24; 5:1). However, this double blessing actually refers to the daily grace and peace which sustains a child of God at all times. Paul began and ended this epistle with an appeal to the grace of God (cf. 6:18). Even though these churches had caused much anxiety, Paul still regarded them as brethren and genuine recipients of divine favor.

The source of this blessing is from two Persons within the divine Being: "God the Father" and "our Lord Jesus Christ."[5] One preposition, "from" (*apo*), links the Father and the Son together as the common source. Doubtless, these gifts are mediated to the believer through the indwelling ministry of

---

[5]The diety of Jesus Christ is affirmed in this verse by the divine title *Lord* (I Cor. 8:6; Phil. 2:11) and by His union with the Father as the common source of grace and peace.

the Holy Spirit. One aspect of the fruit of the Spirit is peace (Gal. 5:22).

## B. A Genuine Message (1:4-5)

A man and his message cannot be separated. Both must be blameless, full of truth, and void of error (I Tim. 2:7).

Paul did not praise a denomination nor did he speak eloquently about philosophy. Rather, he preached Jesus Christ. The apostle declared His Person (who He was) and His work (what He had done). Peter rightfully exclaimed: "Neither is there salvation in any other: for there is none other name under heaven given among men, whereby we must be saved" (Acts 4:12). Four characteristics of this message are set forth here.

### 1. It Involves Substitution (1:4a)

Christ "gave himself for our sins." The basic essence of love is to give. It is overwhelming to realize that "God so loved the world that he gave his only begotten son . . ." (John 3:16). This gift was historic and final. The usage of the past tense ("gave") shows that the gift occurred once and for all at the cross.[6] It can never be repeated (Heb. 9:25-28; 10:12). In every chapter the fact and the value of the cross are stressed (2:20; 3:1, 13; 4:5; 5:11; 6:12-14).

Since the nature of love is giving, the greatest gift is that of self. Christ gave *Himself!* He said to His disciples the night before His crucifixion, "Greater love hath no man than this, that a man lay down his life for his friends" (John 15:13). As the Good Shepherd, He gave His life for the sheep (John 10:11). His sacrificial love for the church provides a model for marital love (Eph. 5:25). God became man, and as the divine-human person, He gave Himself for sinful humanity.

Vicarious atonement is seen in the phrase "for our sins." He died for sins and for sinners (Rom. 5:8). God the Father "made him to be sin for us" (II Cor. 5:21). He did not become a sinner

---

[6]The words "who gave" translate the articular aorist participle *tou dontos.*

on the cross; rather, he became the sin bearer, the divine Passover Lamb who took away the sin of the world (John 1:29; I Cor. 5:7). In His death Christ propitiated God (Rom. 3:25; I John 2:2). He completely satisfied the righteous demands of God for sin. As the infinite, eternal Son of God, He suffered the infinite, eternal penalty for sin during his hours on the cross. The time of sin-bearing was marked by the time of darkness and by His cry: "My God, my God, why hast thou forsaken me?" (Matt. 27:46). It ended when He triumphantly exclaimed, "It is finished" (John 19:30). This final expression (*tetelestai*)[7] shows that Christ had completely and permanently paid the price for the redemption of sinful men. He did not take the sins into the grave or into Hades. His substitutionary suffering occurred only on the cross.

### 2. It Involves Deliverance (1:4b)

Christ died not to improve us, but to rescue us. The purpose of His death is seen in the phrase, "... that he might deliver us...." The verb "deliver" (*exelētai*) literally means "to lift up out of."[8] It is used elsewhere for the plucking out of the right eye which offends (Matt. 5:29), for the deliverance of Joseph from his afflictions (Acts 7:10), for the redemption of Israel out of Egypt (Acts 7:34), for the angelic release of Peter out of the prison of Herod Agrippa I (Acts 12:11), and for the rescue of Paul from Jewish hostility by the Romans (Acts 23:27).

The area of deliverance is "from this present evil world." The word *world* is literally "age" (*aiōnos*). Although the believing sinner has been redeemed from the future judgment of the lake of fire, he has also been rescued from the present satanic world system. The unsaved walk according to the course of this age (Eph. 2:2) and are blinded to the gospel by Satan, the god of this age (II Cor. 4:4). The promise of abundant life includes the presence of spiritual victory, joy, and peace in the midst of moral hostility (John 10:10; 16:33). Christ assured Paul at his

[7]This verb is perfect passive indicative. In business matters it referred to a bill which was paid in full.

[8]It is the aorist middle subjunctive form of *exaireō*.

conversion, "Delivering thee from the people, and from the Gentiles, unto whom now I send thee" (Acts 26:17). This evil age is made up of unregenerate men. This deliverance is the fulfillment of Christ's prayer to keep us from the evil one (John 17:15).

### 3. It Involves the Will of God (1:4c)

The Son became man and entered the world to do the will of God (Heb. 10:7). As He approached the time of His crucifixion, He prayed, ". . . not as I will, but as thou wilt" (Matt. 26:39). God is not willing that any should perish, but He will not impose salvation upon an unwilling heart (Matt. 23:37; I Tim. 2:4; II Peter 3:9). Those who do come to the Savior are then kept by Christ in obedience to the will of the Father (John 6:37–40). The complete plan of redemption is "according to the purpose of him who worketh all things after the counsel of his own will" (Eph. 1:11).

### 4. It Involves the Glory of God (1:5)

The mention of God should always bring forth praise. Salvation is basically theocentric, not anthropocentric. Through the plan of redemption God has gained infinitely more than man. The cross of Jesus Christ is the greatest display of divine love, grace, mercy, and forgiveness. On the night before the crucifixion, the Savior prayed, "Father, the hour is come; glorify thy Son, that thy Son also may glorify thee" (John 17:1).

To bring glory to God a believer must thank Him for who He is and for what He has done. He must admit, with Jonah, that "salvation is of the Lord" (Jonah 2:9). He does that when he knows that the plan, provision, gift, and preservation of human redemption is all of God. This is the reason why Paul concluded his book with these words: "But God forbid that I should glory, save in the cross of our Lord Jesus Christ" (Gal. 6:14).

When a person adds works to faith as a prerequisite to salvation or as a basis for the retention of salvation, he takes away from the glory of God. To Paul the difference between a true gospel and a false message was determined by whether God received all of the glory or just part of it. Evolutionists strip the glory of creation away from God, and the Judaizers were stealing the glory of redemption from Him.

## II. THE WARNING AGAINST PERVERSION (1:6-9)

God's workers have always stood with a shovel in one hand and a sword in the other (Neh. 4:17-18); they must build and defend at the same time. Paul likewise evangelized lost sinners and warned the converts about false teachers (cf. Acts 20:28-31). To preach all the counsel of God is to do both (Acts 20:27).

### A. His Surprise (1:6-7)

The opening verb "I marvel" marks the abrupt change from the presentation of the true gospel to a warning about a false gospel. The customary prayer of thanksgiving is conspicuous by its absence.

#### 1. At Their Transfer (1:6)

He was amazed at their "soon" removal. This does not mean that he did not expect them to change, but that he did not expect it to happen so fast. Spiritual babes are very susceptible to error, and Paul knew that heresy would invade the churches after he left (Acts 20:29-30; Eph. 4:14). The Galatians quickly acquiesced without much resistance to the false teachers shortly after their arrival in the churches. These Galatian converts were very submissive to God; consequently the Judaizers took advantage of their willingness and ignorance to produce a radical departure. The believers doubtless thought that they were obeying God fully. The apostle decided to shock them severly.

The verb ("ye are removed") indicates that they were in the process of being transferred.[9] They had succumbed to a

---

[9]The verb *metatithesthe* is in the present tense. It could be either in the middle or the passive voice. If the former, it means that they were removing themselves or permitting themselves to be changed. If the latter, it means that they were being changed by an outside influence.

ritualistic calendar of observance (4:10), but they had not yet submitted to the necessity of circumcision (5:2). They were like people moving from New York to California who had not yet crossed the Mississippi River. Paul believed that he could stop them before it was too late (5:10).

They were being transferred from a person to a position ("from him that called you into the grace of Christ unto another gospel"). It was not like a Methodist becoming a Baptist. They were going from the true God to a false gospel. God called the Galatians in "grace" (Rom. 8:30).[10] The usage of the past tense reveals Paul's conviction that they were genuinely saved when he evangelized their cities.[11] The grace calling shows that they did not deserve it, but they still received it. Grace becomes a dominant theme within the epistle (1:3, 6, 15; 2:9, 21; 5:4; 6:18).

### 2. At Their Ignorance (1:7)

Through satanic subtlety their minds had been "corrupted from the simplicity that is in Christ" (II Cor. 11:3). They had become unaware of three facts. *First,* they did not know that the message of the Judaizers was a different gospel. The adjective "another" appears twice, but actually it is the translation of two different Greek words: ". . . unto another [*heteron*] gospel: which is not another [*allo*]." This is a play on words through the synonyms. The first refers to another of a different kind, whereas the second refers to another of the same kind. For example: A boy, who ate some fruit (McIntosh apple), was given another or different fruit (Bartlett pear), which was not another (Delicious apple). Paul warned the Corinthians against receiving "another [*heteron*] spirit, which ye have not received, or another [*heteron*] gospel, which ye have not accepted" (II Cor. 11:4).

*Second,* they did not know that the false teachers were actually confusing them mentally and spiritually ("there be some

---

[10]The preposition "into" is literally "in" (*en*).

[11]The phrase "him that called" is the translation of the articular aorist participle *tou kalesantos.*

that trouble you"). The false teachers did this by casting suspicion on Paul's apostleship and by putting pressure on the Galatians to change their theological position. These troublemakers ("some") had a strong leader who led the attack against the apostle (5:10). It was a contemporary, continuous onslaught.[12] Later the apostles and the church at Jerusalem warned against such heretics: "Forasmuch as we have heard, that certain which went out from us have troubled you with words, subverting your souls, saying, Ye must be circumcised and keep the law: to whom we gave no such commandment" (Acts 15:24).

*Third,* they did not know that the Judaizers had actually changed the gospel message. The phrase literally reads, ". . . who are willing to pervert the gospel of Christ." They knew what they were doing when they deliberately chose to change completely the gospel of grace into a message of legalism. The heretics knew the facts of the real gospel but they voluntarily repudiated them. When works are added to faith as the basis of divine justification, the gospel has been changed. Faith in Christ alone saves; any other means will lead a person to damnation (Prov. 14:12; Matt. 5:20).

## B. His Warning (1:8-9)

The message validates the messenger, not vice versa. Paul now applied this scriptural principle to a hypothetical situation and to a factual one.

### 1. To Angels and to Himself (1:8)

This hypothetical warning is introduced by the word "though" (*ean*).[13] The emphatic pronoun "we" would include Paul, Barnabas, and possibly the brethren at Antioch (1:2). The "angel from heaven" would refer to a holy angel, not to a fallen angel nor a satanic substitute (cf. II Cor. 11:13-15). No

[12]The verb "trouble" is a present active participle.
[13]The conditional clause has *ean* ("if" or "though") with the subjunctive mood.

believer should be impressed with the outward qualifications of a person; what he says is what really counts. False prophets, through their oratory and superhuman works, can easily deceive a sinful world and confuse the saved (Matt. 24:11, 24). Paul was not awed by people who had a reputation (2:2, 4, 6).

The standard of judgment must be the message of redemptive grace ("any other gospel unto you than that which we have preached unto you"). The word *than* literally means "beside" (*para*). The evangelistic sermon of any preacher must match the Pauline gospel exactly; it cannot parallel or approximate it. No foundation for salvation can be laid other than the person and redemptive work of Jesus Christ (I Cor. 3:11). Paul assured the Galatians that they heard from his lips the full gospel; nothing was added or left out.

Any preacher who proclaims a false gospel will be "accursed" (*anathema*). This word applies to destruction, both physical death and eternal death in the lake of fire. Paul's enemies placed themselves under a curse (*anathema*) in order to seek the murder of the apostle (Acts 23:12, 14, 21). Paul was willing to be "accursed from Christ" if the entire nation of Israel could be saved through his surrender of eternal life (Rom. 9:37). The *anathema* rests on those who do not love Christ (I Cor. 16:22). No believer would ever claim that Christ was accursed (I Cor. 12:3).

### 2. To the Heretics (1:9)

Such false preaching was actually going on in the Galatian church at the time the apostle wrote the letter.[14] The usage of the indefinite pronoun "any" (*tis*) stresses the point that it doesn't matter who does it. Such a person, whether known or unknown, comes under the divine curse. The singular "any" refers to a personal denial, rather than a corporate rejection of the truth and probably points to the leader of the Judaizing group (5:10).

---

[14]The conditional clause has "if" (*ei*) with the present indicative verb. The phrase literally reads, "If any man is preaching any other gospel to you, and someone is doing just that...."

Paul's warning of judgment was stated by both Barnabas and him in their missionary approach to the Galatians ("as we said before"), and is now being repeated for their spiritual exhortation ("so say I now again").

The true gospel must have total truth within it. It cannot have a mixture of truth and error, no matter what the percentage of error might be. Whenever anyone adds any work (e.g. circumcision, baptism, church membership) to faith as the means of securing divine justification, then he has begun to proclaim a gospel which is beside that which Paul declared.

## QUESTIONS FOR DISCUSSION

1. Are there any biblical apostles today? What would you say or do if someone claimed to be an apostle in your church?
2. Is there any difference between divine and human ordination? Are modern ordination councils scriptural?
3. How can we tell whether a person has been called of God into full-time Christian service? What authentication should we seek?
4. Can a divorced man become a pastor? Should churches ordain women? Should there be any academic qualifications for the pastorate? College? Seminary?
5. When a church is looking for a pastor what questions should be asked of the candidate? Should both the officers and the membership ask these questions?
6. What false gospels are being preached today? What areas of denial are the most important?
7. Are contemporary evangelicals afraid to label certain preachers as heretics? What causes this reluctance? Is this why some denominations have become tainted with liberalism?

# 2

# *The Divine Origin of Paul's Gospel*
## *Galatians 1:10–24*

In his opening remarks Paul claimed that his apostleship did not have human origin, but that it came directly from God (1:1). After exalting the redemptive work of Jesus Christ (1:4–5), he then pronounced a divine curse on anyone who would preach a false gospel (1:6–9). In the second half of this first chapter he will defend himself against the untrue accusations of his critics. They not only denied that he was a genuine apostle, but they also boasted that Paul was indebted to other men for the actual content of his preaching. This criticism had to be repudiated.

## I. HIS MESSAGE CAME FROM GOD (1:10–16a)

The authority of men sent from God has always been questioned by dubious skeptics. The Pharisees rejected the credentials of John the Baptist to preach and to baptize (John 1:19–25). The priests asked Jesus in the temple, "By what authority doest thou these things? and who gave thee this authority?" (Matt. 21:23). John and Jesus declared that their messages came from heaven, not from earthly men. In the same way Paul was attacked, and in the same way he responded.

### A.  His Present Confession (1:10–12)

The connective "for" (*gar*) joins the two sections. The Judaizers charged that Paul preached a partial gospel (faith *without* circumcision and legal obedience), and he denounced them for declaring a heretical message (faith *plus* circumcision and legal obedience). They claimed that Paul tried to please the Gentiles by omitting the necessity of circumcision. In rebuttal the apostle alleged that they were pleasing the Jews by requiring Mosaic rites.

### 1. He Served Only Christ (1:10)

In a series of two questions he denied that he attempted to please men with his sermons. They both raised the issue of his motivation. The *first* dealt with his present attitude. Did he seek to win the approval ("persuade") of men or God? The harsh language which he had just used showed that he was not a men-pleaser (cf. 1:6–9). He did attempt to persuade sinners and rebellious Christians to be reconciled to God, but he did that in order to gain divine approval of his ministry at the judgment seat of Christ (II Cor. 5:10–11). However, he did not tell men what they wanted to hear but only that which they needed to hear. The cultural and religious backgrounds of his listeners did not affect the content of his message. It was always the same. He once wrote, "For the Jews require a sign, and the Greeks seek after wisdom: But we preach Christ crucified, unto the Jews a stumblingblock, and unto the Greeks foolishness" (I Cor. 1:22–23).

Paul adapted his method of evangelization but never his message to his audience. With compassion he exclaimed, "I am made all things to all men, that I might by all means save some" (I Cor. 9:22). To the pagans he referred to the God of creation (Acts 14:15–17), and to the Jews he pointed to the revelation of God in the Old Testament (Acts 13:14–41), but his message always centered in redemption through faith in Jesus Christ.

The *second* question pointed to his future aspirations ("do I seek to please men?"). The outward evaluation of his ministry by men did not disturb Paul (I Cor. 4:3–5). He encouraged slaves to perform their duties to God even when their earthly masters were not watching (Eph. 6:6, Col. 3:22). In the same attitude he obeyed and served God, not men (cf. Acts 5:29). He welcomed divine scrutiny: "But as were allowed of God to be put in trust with the gospel, even so we speak: not as pleasing men, but God, which trieth our hearts" (I Thess. 2:4).

Paul then admitted that he was once a men-pleaser, but that he no longer was ("for if I yet pleased men"). As a law-loving Pharisee, he desired to please his superiors. His conversion radically changed that purpose. No man can be a pleaser of men and a "servant of Christ" at the same time.[1] No man can serve two masters. No person can preach what Christ wants him to proclaim and what unregenerate man wants him to say. Before men Paul was an apostle (1:1), but before Christ he was a servant.

## 2. *He Received His Message Only from Christ (1:11-12)*

Although Paul severely criticized the Galatians, he still regarded them as "brethren" (cf. 4:12, 5:11, 13; 6:1, 18). He identified them with the brethren who were with him (1:2). He now wanted to certify (literally "make known," (*gnōrizō*) to them four assertions about his message. Three of these are negative denials, and the fourth is a positive claim.

*First,* the gospel[2] which he preached was not according to a human standard ("after man"). Literally it reads "according to man" (*kata anthrōpon*). His message was contrary to what mankind, in itself, would preach to a needy world. The world would declare the necessity of social and economic revolution, of moral reformation, and of international brotherhood. Like Cain who despised the way of blood sacrifice (Gen. 4:1-7), man believes that he can gain the favor of God through his own achievements. Like the rebels at Babel, man feels that he can build a bridge to heaven based on his effort and pride (Gen. 11:1-4). Man actually falls under the indictment of Solomon: "There is a way which seemeth right unto a man, but the end thereof are the ways of death" (Prov. 14:12).

---

[1]The last phrase shows a condition contrary to fact. It is introduced by *ei* and uses secondary tenses in both the protasis and the apodosis.

[2]The noun "gospel" (*euaggelion*) and the verb "preached" (*euaggelisthen*) come from the same root.

All of the world's religions created by man emphasize the necessity of human works for salvation. They all say, "Do," but biblical Christianity says, "Done." The wisest of men never would have imagined the divine plan of redemption (I Cor. 1:21-25; 2:9). The gospel came by divine revelation, not by human creation.

The next two denials actually explain the meaning of the human standard.

*Second,* he did not receive his message from any human source ("of man"). The Galatians had received the gospel from Paul (1:9). They were indebted to him for the content of truth, but the apostle was not obligated to any believer for his knowledge of the redemptive plan. Although Paul heard Stephen preach before the latter's martyrdom, the apostle was not indebted to this faithful deacon for the details of his declarations (Acts 7:54-60). Although Ananias was the first Christian to have contact with the recently converted Paul, Ananias did not tell the apostle what to preach (Acts 9:10-19). Not even Barnabas contributed to Paul's knowledge of the divine mysteries. He denied that he received any spiritual truth from any man in either oral or written form.

Contrariwise, he expected his converts to obey what they had received from him, either in his oral preaching or through his epistles (1:9; I Cor. 11:23; 15:1; Phil. 4:9; I Thess. 2:13; 4:1; II Thess. 3:6). Throughout his ministry he exhorted, "Therefore, brethren, stand fast and hold the traditions which ye have been taught, whether by word, or our epistle" (II Thess. 2:15). These "traditions" were not theological concepts passed down from one generation to another; rather, Paul received them directly from God and he delivered them directly to his spiritual children.[3]

*Third,* he was never taught by any other apostle or believer ("neither was I taught it"). He taught others. He encouraged others who were taught by him to teach the next generation (II

[3]The word *traditions* (*paradosesis*) is based upon the verb "delivered" (*paredōka;* I Cor. 15:3).

Tim. 2:2). In Damascus, Jerusalem, and Antioch he met other prophets and teachers, but they never instructed him. In his former life he had been taught by the revered Gamaliel "according to the perfect manner of the law of the fathers" (Acts 22:3). His knowledge of the content of the Old Testament came through the agency of man, but no man revealed to him the truth of the thirteen epistles which he penned.[4]

*Fourth,* he claimed that he was taught directly by Jesus Christ ("but by the revelation of Jesus Christ").[5] Christ appeared to him as he was on the road to Damascus to apprehend Christians (Acts 9:3–6; 26:12–19).[6] This appearance produced his salvation. Later Christ appeared to him, perhaps in Damascus, Arabia, and Tarsus. At this time the Savior revealed truth directly to Paul and caused him to understand completely the content of that disclosure. Actually his apostleship and message were given to him at the same time.

## B. His Past Conduct (1:13–14)

Throughout his ministry Paul incorporated his personal testimony into a presentation of the gospel (cf. Acts 26:4–21). He did not hide his past from his audience. He told them about his religious zeal as a young Pharisee and what it caused him to do. In his first missionary journey, he had informed the Galatians of these facts: "For ye have heard of my conversation [literally 'behavior'] in time past" (1:13a). However, he never played up his past in order to get a crowd. If he had he would have been a men-pleaser. Rather, he used his past as an illustration of the futility of a man who tried to earn his salvation by good works through obedience to the Mosaic law and Jewish ritualism.

[4]Fourteen books, if Paul wrote Hebrews.

[5]A strong adversative *alla* ("but") is used to show the contrast between human and divine origin.

[6]The words "of Jesus Christ" are a grammatical subjective genitive. It was a revelation by Christ, not about Him.

## 1. He Hated the Church (1:13b)

He viewed the Christian community as a heretical sect that needed to be utterly destroyed. In his unregenerate blindness he saw no compatibility between Jewish Christians and law-obeying Jews. In retrospect, he now recognized that he had actually attacked "the church of God." What exactly is the church? After the rejection of Christ by Israel's leaders became evident, He announced: "I will build my church." (Matt. 16:18).[7] The church is later described as the body of Christ (I Cor. 12:13; Eph. 1:22-23; 4:4; 5:29-32). The church then is composed of born-again people, those who are mystically and spiritually identified with Jesus Christ through their belief in Him as God and their acceptance of His redemptive work for them through His death and resurrection. Since the baptism in the Holy Spirit is necessary for entrance into the body of Christ, the church did not begin until after the ascension of Christ and the descent of the Spirit on the day of Pentecost (I Cor. 12:13 cf. John 15:26; Acts 2:1-4). In this age Christ has identified Himself with His people. To Paul He declared, ". . . why persecutest thou me?" (Acts 9:4). Thus the word "me" is equivalent to the phrase "the church of God."[8] Believers are in Christ (II Cor. 5:17), and Christ is in believers (2:20; Col. 1:27); thus Christ and believers are forever wedded together.

Paul manifested his hatred of the church in two ways. He "persecuted" and "wasted" it. The former refers to the arrests, beatings, and killings of people whereas the latter points to the elimination of Christian doctrine.[9] The two verbs actually reveal that these actions were part of his constant lifestyle.[10]

The Book of Acts bears testimony to his terrible deeds. He

[7]Here is a proof for the deity of Christ. The church of God is the same as "my church," or the church of Christ. Thus Christ is God.

[8]The church of God thus was in existence before the conversion of Paul. This fact has often been denied and neglected by ultradispensationalism.

[9]In a later verse (1:23) this contrast can be seen clearly. The believers remarked that Paul persecuted them ("us") and that he destroyed (same word as "wasted") the faith.

[10]Both are in the imperfect tense. This refers to continuous action in past time. He was persecuting and wasting all the time.

oversaw the stoning of Stephen, the first Christian martyr (7:58—8:1). He imprisoned both men and women in Jerusalem (26:10). He received permission from the high priest to seize Christians who were in the synagogue at Damascus and to bring them bound back to Jerusalem (9:1-2). He was described as a fanatic, "breathing out threatenings and slaughter against the disciples of the Lord" (9:1). Believers were deathly afraid of him (9:10-14, 26). His reputation as the chief persecutor of Christians was widespread, known by both the saved and the unsaved (9:21; 22:3-5, 19-20).

He did it "beyond measure"; he went beyond the call of duty. His fanatical hatred drove him into a frenzy. To Herod Agrippa II he summarized his passion:

> I verily thought with myself, that I ought to do many things contrary to the name of Jesus of Nazareth. Which thing I also did in Jerusalem: and many of the saints did I shut up in prison, having received authority from the chief priests; and when they were put to death, I gave my voice against them. And I punished them oft in every synagogue, and compelled them to blaspheme; and *being exceedingly mad against them,* I persecuted them even unto strange cities (Acts 26:9-11, emphases mine).

His physical oppression of Christians actually went beyond the counsel of his teacher Gamaliel. The elderly doctor of the law had cautioned the religious council against any bodily violence toward the new movement (Acts 5:34-39). However, it is a known maxim that students are more radical than their professors.

His pharisaical love for the law drove Paul to persecute the church. Although he did it "ignorantly in unbelief," he still did it (I Tim. 1:13). In the same manner, their devotion to the law had led the Judaizers to attack the apostleship and message of Paul.

## 2. *He Loved the Traditions (1:14)*

Without any sense of pride he objectively set forth three undisputed facts about his prior life as a Pharisee (Acts 26:4, 5;

Phil. 3:5). *First,* he was advancing rapidly through the ranks of Judaism. The verb "profited" literally means "was cutting before" (*proekopton*). He was like a driver on a crowded highway who keeps advancing by cutting in on other traffic. He was in a hurry to reach his destination, the very top of phariseeism.

*Second,* he was advancing faster than any other person of his age ("above many my equals in mine own nation"). He craved recognition for his religious achievements. In a sense, he was engaged in competition with his ritualistic classmates. He wanted to excel over them in every area: knowledge of the Old Testament and of the oral and written traditions, and religious deeds. His greatest pride was centered in his persecution of the church. He had no equal in this area. Jesus warned the apostles concerning the time when "whosoever killeth you will think that he doeth God service" (John 16:2). Paul epitomized that prediction.

*Third,* he was "more exceedingly zealous of the traditions of [his] fathers." He was at the head of the class. He loved the law in his unsaved past more than any other Pharisee and more than any other Judaizer in the present. In a sense, he was the best religious man who has ever lived. If any person could have gained heaven through his ecclesiastical effort, Paul would have been that man. He later confessed:

> Though I might also have confidence in the flesh. If any other man thinketh that he hath whereof he might trust in the flesh, I more: circumcised the eighth day, of the stock of Israel, of the tribe of Benjamin, an Hebrew of the Hebrews; as touching the law, a Pharisee; concerning zeal, persecuting the church; touching the righteousness which is in the law, blameless (Phil. 3:4–6).

The "traditions" doubtless included the oral and written interpretations and declarations that grew out of an application of the Mosaic law to contemporary life. Unfortunately these human commandments often contradicted and supplanted the divine imperatives. Christ condemned these false requirements (Mark 7:1–23). According to one rabbinical tradition,

"The Scriptures are water; the Mishnah, wine; but the Gemera, spiced wine."[11] The latter two groups form the Talmud, the official interpretation of the Mosaic law.

## C. His Personal Conversion (1:15-16a)

Paul deserved to be condemned forever in the lake of fire, but God "pleased" (*eudokēsen*) to save him. He obtained divine mercy, grace, and love even though he was "a blasphemer, and a persecutor, and injurious" (I Tim. 1:13). He knew that no amount of legal obedience could have rescued him from his standing of spiritual death and guilt. The pleasure of God is seen in the sovereign plan of redemption, decreed in eternity past according to the counsel of divine will (Eph. 1:11), graciously provided through the crucifixion and resurrection of Christ, and executed by the convicting, regenerating ministry of the Holy Spirit (John 3:5; 16:8-11). Four specific acts of God in the life of the apostle are now enumerated.

### 1. God Separated Him (1:15b)

He was "separated [*aphorisas*]... from [his] mother's womb." The verb "separated" means to mark off from a boundary. He confessed that he was "called to be an apostle, separated unto the gospel of God" (Rom. 1:1). He was called to a position, but he was separated to a ministry. The Holy Spirit commanded the prophets and teachers at Antioch: "Separate me Barnabas and Saul for the work whereunto I have called them" (Acts 13:2). Thus the Spirit was the divine agent of separation in preparing Paul from his infancy and in guiding him out of the local church.

The word for "separate" (*aphorisas*) is related to the verb "predestinate" (*proorisas*). Believers are predestined to the adoption of full sonship, the event when they become totally conformed to the image of Christ (Eph. 1:5). They are also separated to a vocational goal within the true church.

Divine separation in time is an evidence of divine selection

[11]R. Alan Cole, *The Epistle of Paul to the Galatians,* p. 50.

in eternity. God said to Jeremiah, "Before I formed thee in the belly I knew thee; and before thou camest forth out of the womb I sanctified thee, and I ordained thee a prophet unto the nations" (Jer. 1:5). John the Baptist was filled with the Holy Spirit from his mother's womb (Luke 1:15). Paul knew that God had providentially set him apart even before his conversion to prepare him as a preacher of the gospel.

### 2. God Called Him (1:15c)

The call of God to salvation is both sovereign and gracious. God "called" (*kalesas*) Paul, and He did it "by his grace." This is not the general invitation to the world to repent; rather, it is the efficacious call of God whereby He graciously secures the assent of man's will to believe. God does not force salvation on an unwilling sinner. Every person that God sovereignly calls will accept Christ as his Savior, but every one who believes does it because he wants to. The call is gracious in that no sinner deserves to be called to salvation. The sinner who has not been efficaciously called has no right to complain because he simply gets what he deserves.

Here is the sequence of the divine plan of redemption: "Moreover whom he did predestinate, them he also called: and whom he called, them he also justified: and whom he justified, them he also glorified" (Rom. 8:30). All who are called by the divine purpose are guaranteed salvation and glorification.

### 3. God Illuminated Him (1:16a)

The purpose of the divine separation and call was "to reveal his Son in [Paul]." On the road to Damascus, Paul and Christ met each other. Through his outward vision of Christ, he became blind; but in his inward experience, he initially recognized Jesus Christ to be the Son of God. It takes divine revelation to know that Jesus is the Christ, the Son of God (Matt. 16:17). The Father sovereignly hides spiritual truth from proud, self-sufficient people, but He reveals such blessings to those who have the attitude of children (Matt. 11:25). Jesus said, "... no man knoweth the Son, but the Father; neither knoweth any man the Father, save the Son, and he to whomsoever the Son will reveal him" (Matt. 11:27).

Such divine illumination occurs within a person's immaterial self and is secured by the Holy Spirit (I Cor. 2:9–12). All believers can say with Paul: "For God ... hath shined in our hearts, to give the light of the knowledge of the glory of God in the face of Jesus Christ" (II Cor. 4:6).

### 4. God Commissioned Him (1:16b)

God directed Paul into a special ministry to the Gentiles ("that I preach him among the heathen").[12] Although he also preached to the Jews, he was known as the apostle to the Gentiles (2:7–9; cf. Rom 1:16; 15:16–21). God explained to Ananias about the conversion of Paul: "Go thy way: for he is a chosen vessel unto me, to bear my name before the Gentiles, and kings, and the children of Israel" (Acts 9:15).

The outreach to the non-Jewish world can be seen in Paul's famous three missionary journeys (Acts 13–21). He was the first apostle to carry the gospel into Europe (Acts 16:10–12). He established more gentile churches than all of the other apostles combined. Whenever he returned to Antioch or Jerusalem he would report "what things God had wrought among the Gentiles by his ministry" (Acts 21:19; cf. 14:27).

## II. HIS MESSAGE DID NOT COME FROM MAN (1:16–24)

This section develops his previously mentioned denial that he received his message from men or that he was taught it by others (1:12). It is a summary of his geographical movements over the next fourteen years during which he had infrequent contacts with the apostles.

[12]The words *heathen* and *Gentiles* refer to the same group (*ethnesin*).

## A. His Conferences (1:16b–20)

### 1. The First Three Years (1:16b–17)

After Paul was converted and blinded by his vision of Christ, he was led to Damascus where he spent three days in the house of Judas (Acts 9:8–11). When his sight was restored he stayed "certain days with the disciples which were at Damascus" (Acts 9:19). This period of time is described as "immediately." In no way did Paul consult with Ananias or any other believer at Damascus about what he should believe, do, or preach. The verb "conferred" (*prosanethemēn*) means to meet someone with a view to be informed on a subject. Paul met several Christians after his conversion, but they did not teach him about doctrinal issues. The phrase "flesh and blood" is an idiom which expresses present human nature (I Cor. 15:50; Heb. 2:14). It generally refers to all mankind, but here it specifically points to genuine believers.

After this brief period at Damascus, he went into "Arabia." This event probably occurred between his postconversion rest at Damascus (Acts 9:19) and his aggressive ministry in the synagogue in that city (Acts 9:20).[13] He made it very clear that he did not return to Jerusalem to consult with the original apostles. In no way did they tell him what to preach either. This Arabia does not correspond to the area around Sinai or to modern Saudi Arabia; rather it refers to the wilderness in the vicinity of Damascus. Doubtless, during his retreat into Arabia, Christ appeared to Paul again and revealed spiritual truth which was completely understood by him through the indwelling ministry of the Holy Spirit. There is no indication that he preached in this desolate area.

He then "returned again unto Damascus." During this second stay he preached in the synagogue to the amazement of all,

[13]Some of the geographical movements mentioned in the Epistles are difficult to harmonize with the Book of Acts. The departure into Arabia may have happened after his first synagogue preaching but before his dramatic escape (Acts 9:20–22; cf. 9:23–25; note the phrase "many days"). Or it could have taken place after his escape through the window in the wall.

was conspired against by the unbelieving Jews, and escaped when he was lowered in a basket through a window in the outside wall. (Acts 9:20–25; II Cor. 11:32–33).

## 2. At Jerusalem (1:18–20)

Three years after his conversion, Paul went to Jerusalem "to see" (*historēsai*) Peter. This verb, used of sightseeing, shows that he wanted to become acquainted with Peter. He did not go to confer with Peter (cf. 1:16). He did not go to receive his apostleship or to be taught by Peter. This visit was rather brief, lasting only "fifteen days."

At this time Paul did not even see the other original apostles who must have been out of the city then. This visit doubtless corresponds to the occasion when Barnabas introduced Paul to the disbelieving disciples in the Jerusalem church who thought that Paul was masquerading his conversion in order to persecute them (Acts 9:26–29). Luke recorded that Paul met the apostles (Acts 9:27), but this is later explained as a reference to just two, namely Peter and James (1:18–19).

He was introduced to James, "the Lord's brother." James was born to Mary and Joseph after the birth of Jesus (Mark 6:3). During Jesus' earthly ministry, James did not accept the messiahship of his half-brother (John 7:5). He became convinced, however, when he saw the recurrected Savior (I Cor. 15:7). During the ten-day interval between the ascension of Christ and the descent of the Holy Spirit, he was in the upper room with the apostles (Acts 1:13, 14). He rapidly rose in prominence and became one of the three main leaders of the Jerusalem church (Acts 12:17; 15:13–23; 21:18–25; Gal. 2:9). The usage of the adjective "other" (*heteron*) shows that his apostleship was gained in a different way than the original twelve. Like Paul, he was converted and commissioned at the same time when he saw the risen Lord.

Paul then affirmed that his testimony about his conferences with believers and apostles after his conversion was absolutely true (1:20). His critics charged him with lying but he called God to be his character witness.

## B. His Absence (1:21-24)

### 1. The Churches in Judea Did Not See Him (1:21-22)

After his abbreviated visit and ministry in Jerusalem, Paul went to the coastal Roman city of Caesarea (Acts 9:30). He proceeded northward up the Mediterranean shore through the provinces of Syria and Cilicia (1:21). He then settled in his home town of Tarsus, where he would spend the next nine years in relative seclusion (Acts 9:30; 11:25).

The churches of Judea, where the apostles labored, never saw Paul (1:22). He "was unknown by face." This truth reinforced his denial of indebtedness to the apostles.

### 2. The Churches in Judea Heard About Him (1:23-24)

These churches had secondary information about his activities ("heard only"). They knew about his past life as a persecutor, his conversion, and his ministry. They accepted these reports as being true. They recognized that Paul "preached the faith which once he destroyed." Since Paul preached justification by faith without circumcision or works, they must have believed in that doctrinal concept also. If the churches of Judea had believed in the necessity of circumcision, as the Judaizers alleged, then those assemblies would have criticized the apostle. Since "they glorified God in [him]", they must have been persuaded that both Paul's apostleship and message were genuine. This type of information could have easily been verified by the Galatians if they wanted to send some representative into the region of Judea.

Paul's claim could be proven objectively. His apostolic ministry came from God, not from man.


## QUESTIONS FOR DISCUSSION

1. In what ways do preachers seek to please men today? Is this men-pleasing a major problem within evangelicalism? Why?
2. What contemporary doctrines and denominations are ac-

cording to man? What is the common ingredient in every heretical gospel?

3. Does Christ reveal Himself to men today? What would you say or do if someone claimed to have seen Christ? Directly? In a vision?

4. Give some examples of people who are involved in racial and religious traditions. How can these people be reached with the gospel?

5. How can the conversion of Paul be used in witnessing to others? Is any sinner beyond hope of salvation?

6. In what ways does God prepare men for salvation and for service? Illustrate from your own experience.

7. Why are believers so quick to accept the criticism of other believers? What can be done to correct this situation?

# 3

# The Recognition of Paul's Gospel
## Galatians 2:1–10

In the first fourteen years of his Christian life Paul had only one brief encounter with Peter and James and none with the entire apostolic band. Although the Judaizers charged that he was indebted to others for his apostolic ministry, there was no objective, historical evidence for that accusation. Near the end of this period of comparative obscurity Barnabas brought Paul from Tarsus in Cilicia to work in the church at Antioch in Syria (Acts 9:30; 11:25-26). Before the start of his first missionary journey (Acts 13:1—14:28) and the subsequent council of Jerusalem (Acts 15:1-29), Paul engaged in two extremely important meetings: one with the apostles in Jerusalem (2:1-10) and the other with Peter in Antioch (2:11-21).[1] In both of these times he defended the integrity of his apostleship and message. In both his apostolic ministry was recognized by the other apostles to be genuine.

## I. IN THE CONVERSION OF TITUS (2:1-5)

There is considerable debate over the exact time of the conference in Jerusalem. The phrase "fourteen years after"[2] can be dated either to the conversion of Paul (A.D. 32) or to the first visit to Jerusalem (1:18; A.D. 35). If it is the former, the meeting

[1]The Antioch experience may have occurred after the missionary journey but before the Jerusalem council.

[2]Literally "through fourteen years."

would correspond to the famine visit in which Paul and Barnabas took a welfare gift to the church at Jerusalem (Acts 11:27–30; A.D. 46).[3] If it is the latter, the discussion would be equivalent to the famous council which dealt with the means of justification (Acts 15:1–29; A.D. 49).[4]

Those who equate the conference of Galatians 2 with that of Acts 15 argue that the doctrinal position of justification by faith apart from circumcision was the main topic of debate, that many of the same people are mentioned (e.g. Paul, Barnabas, Peter, and James), and that there were probably three meetings in Acts 15: two public and one private. The private meeting could have happened between the two public conferences (cf. Acts 15:6).

The proponents who equate this passage with the famine relief visit (Acts 11:27–30) point out that Paul would have quoted from the decree instituted at the council of Jerusalem if he had actually written the book after that critical decision (Acts 15:7–20; cf. 15:24). Since the apostle rehearsed his various contacts with the Jerusalem apostles, he had to mention the famine visit in which both Barnabas and he participated. The adverb "again" shows that this was his second visit to that great city. Any omission of any visit would have been used by his critics against him. Although both views have some problems of chronological harmony within them, the second view seems more likely. In either case, the verdict of the debate remains unchanged.

## A. People at the Meeting (2:1)

In addition to himself Paul mentioned two others who went with him: Barnabas, his friend and missionary associate, and Titus, a pure Gentile convert.

---

[3]Held by Homer A. Kent, *The Freedom of God's Sons,* p. 53, Merrill F. Tenney, *New Testament Survey,* p. 268, and this author.

[4]Held by Herman N. Ridderbos, *The Epistle of Paul to the Churches of Galatia,* p. 76, and A. T. Robertson, *Word Pictures in the New Testament,* IV, 282.

## 1. Barnabas

His real name was Joses, but he was surnamed *Barnabas* by the apostles in Jerusalem (Acts 4:36). This name means "son of consolation." He was a Levite, a member of the priestly tribe, and a resident of the island of Cyprus. When the church had a financial need, he sold his land and brought the sale money to the apostles (Acts 4:37).

He formally introduced Paul to the church after the latter's dramatic conversion (Acts 9:27). When the Jerusalem church heard about the gospel outreach in Syrian Antioch, it sent Barnabas to oversee the work (Acts 11:19-24). He then went to Tarsus and brought Paul back to Antioch to work with him (Acts 11:25-26). Later the Antioch church sent financial relief to Jerusalem via Barnabas and Paul (Acts 11:29-30). When they returned to Antioch they took John Mark, the nephew of Barnabas (Acts 12:25; Col. 4:10).

Barnabas was with Paul for the entire first missionary journey (Acts 13:1—14:28). He went with Paul to the council at Jerusalem to defend the message which they both preached (Acts 15:1-35). After their return to Antioch, Paul and he engaged in a dispute over the wisdom of taking John Mark on the second missionary journey (Acts 15:36-41). This event led to a separation between Paul and him. From this point on, the Book of Acts is silent about Barnabas's activities.

## 2. Titus

Titus was a full Greek by ancestry. Since Paul called him "mine own son after the common faith" (Titus 1:4), he was probably converted under the apostle's ministry, perhaps at Syrian Antioch.

Although his name is not mentioned in the Book of Acts, he was with Paul during the latter's third missionary journey. Paul sent him to Corinth from Ephesus to deal with the delicate problems there (II Cor. 2:13; 7:6-16). His ministry was successful, and he returned to Paul in Macedonia with the good report. The apostle then sent Titus back to Corinth with the Epistle of II Corinthians.

The Bible is silent as to whether Titus was with Paul during the latter's imprisonments in Caesarea and Rome. However, he was with Paul during the interval between the two Roman imprisonments. Paul took him to Crete and left him there in charge of the work (Titus 1:5). Later the apostle wanted Titus to rejoin him at Nicopolis, but it is difficult to say whether he did just that (Titus 3:12). He was with Paul shortly before the apostle's martyrdom, because he left Rome for Dalmatia (II Tim. 4:10).

Of course, one inspired book was addressed to him.

## B. Purpose of the Meeting (2:2)

### 1. To Present a Gentile Convert

Paul deliberately "took Titus" along as a graphic exhibit of a Gentile who was saved by faith in Christ without the rite of physical circumcision. Titus' life and character must have manifested spiritual depth at that time; otherwise the apostle would not have brought him. It appears that the church at Jerusalem had never met a convert out of a total pagan, idolatrous background before this confrontation.

### 2. To Set Forth the Gospel Message

The trip was made "by revelation." God directed the apostle to take this historic pilgrimage. The fact of revelation is certain, but its means is unclear. Three possibilities exist. *First,* it could have been a direct disclosure through a vision (Acts 16:9), an angelic visitation (Acts 27:23–24), or a divine vocal message (Acts 9:4). *Second,* God could have spoken by the Holy Spirit to the entire church at Antioch. He so commanded the church to send Paul and Barnabas on their first missionary journey (Acts 13:1–4). *Third,* the revelation may refer to the pronouncement of Agabus who prophesied by the Spirit that a famine would occur (Acts 11:27–30). This declaration of divine direction shows that Paul was not forced by Antioch or Jerusalem to go to this meeting. The apostles did not call him into account. Paul did not report as an inferior to his superior.

He "communicated [anethemēn] unto them the gospel." This

verb means that he declared or laid before them his message for their consideration. He did not go to find out what to preach or to be corrected. The additional phrase ("which I preach among the Gentiles") shows that Paul declared in the Jerusalem conference the same message that he was presently preaching when he wrote the book.[5] His gospel had not vacillated in the slightest from the time that he had received it directly from Christ.

This disclosure took place in a special private meeting attended by the recognized spiritual leaders of the Jerusalem congregation ("privately"). The descriptive phrase "to them which were of reputation" literally means "to the ones who seem to be" (*tois dokousi*).[6] It occurs three times (2:2, 6, 9). It definitely includes Peter, John, and James and it could also refer to the other apostles and elders (Acts 15:6). It is possible that it could embrace that group of levitical priests and Pharisees who were saved in the early days of persecution (Acts 6:7; 15:5).

The preference of a private meeting over a public one was to eliminate the danger of public misunderstanding over any theological differences that might surface. He knew that his gospel was true but he was concerned enough to check it out. He did not want to be in error and he did not want them to be in error. There is only "one faith" (Eph. 4:5), and the two groups had to be sure that both were preaching the same gospel. If the Jerusalem apostles had unanimously disagreed with Paul's message, he would have had to question his interpretation of his ministry ("lest by any means I should run, or had run, in vain"). Much later Apollos who preached a true but incomplete message was led into "the way of God more perfectly" by Aquila and Priscilla (Acts 18:24–26). Paul was willing to subject his message and his convert Titus to this careful apostolic scrutiny. Thus his critics could never prove that he acted independently or recklessly.

[5]The verb "preach" (*kērussō*) is in the present tense.

[6]The heresy of Docetic Gnosticism took its name from this verb. This apostate group taught that Christ appeared to have a real human body but that He did not.

## C. Pressure at the Meeting (2:3-5)

### 1. Upon Titus (2:3)

Titus was not "compelled to be circumcised." If the Jerusalem apostles had believed in the necessity of circumcision for salvation, they would have forced that rite upon the Gentile Titus. This would have been the logical time and place for them to have expressed their convictions, since they were in a Jewish city and in a Jewish church where all of the members had been circumcised before their salvation experience.

From whom then did the pressure come? Some "false brethren" revealed their private beliefs publicly. At the council of Jerusalem "there rose up certain of the sect of the Pharisees which believed, saying, That it was needful to circumcise them, and to command them to keep the law of Moses" (Acts 15:5). Doubtless, these reflected the sentiments of other professing Christians from Judea who exclaimed to the Gentiles, "Except ye be circumcised after the manner of Moses, ye cannot be saved" (Acts 15:1). The pressure then came from Jewish members of the Jerusalem church who professed faith in Christ but who also believed that circumcision was necessary. To them it did not matter whether the rite was performed at infancy, at a Gentile's introduction into Judaism as a proselyte, or after a confession of faith by a pagan Gentile. To them it *had* to be done to gain justification.

### 2. Upon Paul (2:4-5)

The pressure placed upon Titus also fell upon Paul. After all, the apostle was the human instrument in the salvation of Titus and he was responsible for bringing the Gentile to Jerusalem.

This pressure group was characterized in five ways. *First,* they were "false brethren." Jesus had followers who were not really saved (John 6:60, 64). Peter warned about the presence of false prophets and false teachers (II Peter 2:1). John predicted the exodus of false believers from within the church (I John 2:18-19). Paul often cautioned churches: "Also of your own selves shall men arise, speaking perverse things, to draw away disciples after them" (Acts 20:30).

*Second,* they were devious ("unawares brought in"). This term (*pareisaktous*) literally means "to lead into beside." This is the same group that preached a gospel "beside" (*para*) that which the Galatians had heard from Paul (1:9). These are the false teachers "who privily shall bring in [same word] damnable heresies" (II Peter 2:1).

*Third,* they were not supposed to be at the meeting. They literally "came into" the conference room "beside" the real apostles (*pareisēlthon*). They slipped in unnoticed. Philipps, in his translation, said that "they wormed their way into our meeting."

*Fourth,* they were critical spies ("to spy out"). The verb (*kataskopēsai*) is used of a spy who goes to a hill to look down upon the camp of the enemy. Their object of sight was "liberty . . . in Christ Jesus." This freedom referred to deliverance from the Mosaic law as a means of justification and sanctification. He later wrote, "Stand fast therefore in the liberty [same word] wherewith Christ hath made us free" (5:1).

*Fifth,* they intended to force Paul and Titus to yield to their pressure ("that they might bring us into bondage"). They saw the apostle as an enemy to be captured or destroyed. They did not enter the meeting with an open mind to learn about Gentile salvation. They were convinced that they were doctrinally right, and they were going to force their convictions upon others.

Paul adamantly resisted this pressure ("to whom we gave place by subjection, no"). He did not vacillate. He did not yield to their demands in the slightest. To him circumcision was not necessary for either Gentile or Jewish salvation. They may have wanted Paul to concede that Jews needed to be circumcised because of their physical relationship to Abraham, but he also saw this concession as a compromise to the gospel message.

He did not entertain the thought of submission for a moment ("no, not for an hour").[7] There was no weakness or hesitation on

---

[7]The negation is more emphatic in the Greek text. The negative *oude* appears second in the verse.

his part. He did not give in partially, and then later retreat to his original position.

He was a man of principle, not of expediency. He defended his theological position for the sake of the gospel, not basically for himself ("that the truth of the gospel might continue with you"). If he had yielded to the pressures of the legalists, the foundation of the Galatian churches would have been weakened and destroyed.

## II. BY THE OTHER APOSTLES (2:6-10)

The apostleship of Paul was denied by false apostles (II Cor. 12:13), but it was never questioned by the genuine apostles of Jerusalem. In turn, Paul never repudiated the apostleship of the original twelve. In this passage the Jerusalem group recognized three qualities about Paul's life and ministry.

### A. He Did Not Need Any Information (2:6)

Throughout this book he affirmed that he received no spiritual truth from any believer. In this sense, he was unique. He did listen to other preachers, but they did not increase his comprehension of any doctrine. As the result of this conference, he stated two facts: he was not influenced by who men were nor by what they knew.

#### 1. Their Status (2:6a)

Others were impressed with the past station of the church leaders at Jerusalem. To others these "seemed to be somewhat" (*tōn dokountōn einai ti*). In the case of Peter and John, this would refer to their close association with Jesus during His earthly ministry. They were not only members of the original band but they were also part of the inner circle of three (Peter, James, and John; cf. Matt. 17:1). James (1:19; 2:9) was the half-brother of Jesus, born to Mary and Joseph. In addition, all three had seen the resurrected Christ and all three were viewed as the three major pillars of the Jerusalem work (2:9). If the descriptive phrase included more than these, it would have doubtless referred to those priests and Pharisees who were now professing believers (Acts 6:7, 15:5). These men who had once offered sacrifices in the temple and who had influential roles in Judaism could have overwhelmed poor Jewish Christians with their mere presence.

Paul, however, was not awed by their past because God was not affected by the cultural background of men. He wrote: ". . . whatsoever they were, it maketh no matter to me: God accepteth no man's person." God is not partial. He did not choose men to salvation or to service because of who they were or what they could do (I Cor. 1:26–31). In fact, Peter, Paul, and James all acknowledged that God is no respecter of persons (Acts 10:34; Rom. 2:11; James 2:1–9).

### 2. *Their Knowledge (2:6b)*

At the conference the apostles did not tell Paul anything that he did not know ("for they who seemed to be somewhat in conference added nothing to me"). He listened and agreed to what they said but his spiritual understanding was not even minutely increased. This is not a statement of bragging but only an affirmation of fact. The verb "added" (*prosanethento*) is the same word as "conferred" (1:16). No man, regardless of his position or intellect, could have added complementary theological concepts to those which Jesus Christ revealed directly to Paul.

## B. He Had a Special Sphere of Ministry (2:7–8)

The next two connective words ("But contrariwise") show that even though the apostles did not add anything to Paul, neither did they take anything away from him. In fact, their recognition of his genuine apostolic ministry erased many possible obstacles to the extension and acceptance of his service to the churches.

### 1. *He Had a Different Audience (2:7)*

The apostles had divinely imparted wisdom and humility to perceive that God had called Paul to be an apostle and that his message was accurate because it was revealed by Christ ("when they saw"). They also recognized that God had led Paul to have a special ministry to the Gentiles and that the same God had commanded Peter to have a unique ministry to the Jews. The two phrases ("the gospel of the uncircumcision" and "the gospel of the circumcision") do not mean that there were two different messages preached to two different racial groups.[8] They do not imply that Paul declared that a Gentile was justified by faith alone and that Peter proclaimed that a Jew was declared righteous by faith plus circumcision. There is only *one* gospel, "one faith" (Eph. 4:5).

In fact, both Paul and Peter preached to Jews and Gentiles alike. Whenever Paul went into a new city during his missionary travels, he always engaged in a synagogue ministry to the Jews and Gentile proselytes before he reached out into the pagan Gentile community. He followed this practice clearly in the Galatian cities (Acts 13:14-45; cf. 13:46-49; 14:1 cf. 14:2). He did not vary the message as the audience changed, although his method of approach differed (cf. I Cor. 9:19-23). It was Paul who wrote that the gospel of Christ was "the power of God unto salvation to everyone that believeth: to the Jew first, and also to the Greek" (Rom. 1:16; cf. 3:22). The burden of Paul, however, was to preach to Gentiles who had never heard, whereas the aim of Peter was to reach his own people.

In modern missions there are agencies whose main purpose is to win Jews, but their missionaries will witness to Gentiles as well. Thus the difference between Paul and Peter was seen to be in the scope of outreach.

### 2. He Had the Same Apostleship (2:8)

Apostles were commissioned by Christ to preach the gospel to all nations (Matt. 28:19; Rom. 1:5). Both Paul and Peter were aware of this mandate.

This conference thus recognized that the same God had

---

[8]The words *uncircumcision* and *circumcision* should be seen as objective genitives. Paul evangelized the uncircumcised Gentiles and Peter evangelized the circumcised Jews.

called both of these key figures ("he" ... "the same"). Both had seen and heard the resurrected Christ.

The council also knew that God had gifted both men and that He had delegated equal authority to them. The two verbs ("wrought effectually" and "was mighty") show that God had energized them. These verbs actually come from the same root word (*energeō*). Although the spheres of ministry were different, their authority was equal. Both were confirmed by miraculous signs and inspired utterances. They were both needed to lay a proper foundation for the church (Eph. 2:20).

Although Paul intensely desired to see Israel saved, he had to confess, "I am the apostle of the Gentiles, I magnify my office" (Rom. 11:13).

### 3. He Was Part of the Fellowship (2:9-10)

In the leadership of the Jerusalem church three men rose to the place of prominence: James, Cephas or Peter,[9] and John. In the original band of apostles the inner circle of Christ's associates was composed of Peter and the brothers, James and John. As the result of the martyrdom of James, the half-brother of Jesus, who was also named James, assumed the position of the dead apostle. Since he is mentioned first in this list, he must be acknowledged as the presiding elder-apostle of the church (cf. 2:12; Acts 15:13). Peter, of course, was the dominant apostle in the early days of church history (Acts 1–12). He preached the first sermon to the Jews after the death, resurrection, and ascension of Christ (Acts 2). He used the keys of the kingdom of heaven again when he proclaimed the gospel to the Gentiles through Cornelius for the first time (Matt. 16:18; Acts 10). Both Peter and John were the instruments of God to impart the Holy Spirit to the believing Samaritans (Acts 8:14–17). John, later, was to write five inspired books (Gospel of John; I, II, III John; and Revelation). Peter wrote two books and James one. Along with Paul these four composed twenty-

[9]The name *Cephas* is Aramaic, whereas *Peter* is Greek. Both mean "rock." These names were given to Simon by Christ.

one of the twenty-seven books within the New Testament.[10] To all concerned, they "seemed to be pillars." Their dominant personalities and abilities definitely supported the work of God in that city. Their decision about Paul, therefore, would have wide influence among the others.

These three unanimously took four steps. *First,* they "perceived the grace that was given" to Paul (2:9a). The verb "perceived" (*gnontes*) indicates that they came to an understanding through this conference with Paul. They learned from Paul about the work of God in Paul's life. They knew that the apostolic ministry was not something that he had taken upon himself or that which others had imparted to him. His salvation and service manifested divine grace. Paul agreed with their conclusion in these words:

> For I am the least of the apostles, that am not meet to be called an apostle, because I persecuted the church of God. But by the grace of God I am what I am: and his grace which was bestowed upon me was not in vain: but I laboured more abundantly than they all: yet not I, but the grace of God which was with me (I Cor. 15:9-10).

*Second,* they gave to Paul and Barnabas "the right of hands of fellowship" (2:9b). The two groups identified themselves with each other in the family of God and in the work of the ministry. This gesture was a sign of friendship and trust. The noun "fellowship" (*koinōnia*) points to that which is shared or that which is common to men and to God (I John 1:3).

*Third,* they agreed on their respective areas of ministry ("that we should go unto the heathen, and they unto the circumcision"; 2:9c). They saw no conflict in what each was doing; there was neither competition nor jealousy. They recognized that they were both doing what God had wanted them to do. They both preached the same message but with different approaches to different people.

*Fourth,* they desired that Paul would give financial support

[10]If Paul wrote Hebrews, then the total would be twenty-two.

to the poor Jewish Christians in Jerusalem (2:10). This was a request, not a demand. The verb "remember" suggests that they wanted the apostle to continue his welfare program which he had already started.[11]   He then indicated that he had already determined to encourage the Gentile Christians to support their Jewish brothers in the Lord ("which I also was forward to do"). Barnabas and Paul had actually made the trip from Antioch to Jerusalem to bring financial relief (Acts 11:29-30). Later, during his third missionary journey, he gave instructions to the churches of Galatia, Macedonia, and Achaia concerning an extremely large welfare offering for the Jerusalem poor (I Cor. 16:1-3). Paul later commented:

> For it hath pleased them of Macedonia and Achaia to make a certain contribution for the poor saints which are at Jerusalem. It hath pleased them verily; and their debtors they are. For if the Gentiles have been made partakers of their spiritual things, their duty is also to minister unto them in carnal things (Rom. 15:26-27).

Consequently, it was not necessary for the apostles to bring up the subject of giving to the poor. Even in this area they added nothing to Paul. He constantly taught his converts, "As we have therefore opportunity, let us do good unto all men, especially unto them who are of the household of faith" (6:10). Personal, financial support of widows, orphans, and the impoverished is at the very center of biblical Christianity (I Tim. 5:3-10; James 1:27).

## QUESTIONS FOR DISCUSSION

1. With whom are evangelicals impressed today? How do such people gain a reputation? What can be done to correct partiality?
2. Are different messages being preached to different people today? Cite some specific illustrations.

[11]The verb "remember" (*mnēmoneuōmen*) is present subjunctive.

3. How can evangelicals use different methods to proclaim the same message? Are preachers unjustly criticized for using various methods?
4. How do false brethren get into the churches? What can be done to prevent their influence from destroying a church?
5. Do Christians have doctrinal convictions today? Are they easily influenced by others? Do some preachers take advantage of the doctrinal weakness of their followers?
6. Are carefully defined ministries, such as to the Jews, to the inner city, to college students, approved by the Scriptures? In what ways should they be incorporated into the life of the local church?
7. Are evangelicals sufficiently concerned over the poor? In their churches? In their cities? in the world? Can too much money be given to the poor?

# 4

# *The Defense of Paul's Gospel*
### *Galatians 2:11–21*

The first two chapters of this inspired book are full of autobiographical references. In defense of his apostleship and message, Paul referred to his unregenerate pharisaical past, to his dramatic conversion, to his travels, to the firm stand taken for his convictions at the Jerusalem council, and now to his confrontation with Peter at Syrian Antioch. These bits of personal history demonstrated that he was adamantly opposed to any alteration of the foundational doctrine that a sinner is justified by faith in Christ alone. His critics charged that he was a weak and vacillating person, but these allegations were contradicted by this historical, objective evidence. Paul stood for the truth in every situation.

## I. CRITICISM OF PETER'S ACTIONS (2:11-14)

At Jerusalem both Paul and Titus were under close scrutiny. The roles became reversed in Antioch, the home church of the famed apostle. Now Peter was to experience rebuke for his practical denial of the oneness in Christ for both Jewish and Gentile believers.

### A. What Paul Sensed in Peter (2:11)

The occasion of this unlikely encounter was Peter's visit to Antioch. The Book of Acts is silent about this trip. After the proceedings in Jerusalem, Peter doubtless wanted to see the work at Antioch firsthand. If that event in Jerusalem was the famine visit of Paul and Barnabas (Acts 11:30), Peter could have traveled to the Gentile city shortly before Paul's first missionary journey started (Acts 12:25—13:2) or after the team returned (Acts 14:26–28).[1] Peter was forced to leave Jerusalem because of the martyrdom of James, his own imprisonment, and his miraculous escape; thus he would have been on the move. If the strategic council at Jerusalem was synonymous with this conference (Acts 15; cf. Gal. 2), then Peter could have gone to Antioch before Paul started out on his second journey (Acts 15:35–36).[2]

Paul's actions must have startled the entire church when he "withstood [Peter] to the face." This was an act of personal courage. The verb "withstood" (*antestēn*) literally means "to stand against." Paul did not keep his mouth shut nor did he whisper behind Peter's back. He rebuked Peter "to the face." The critics charged that Paul's letters were "weighty and powerful, but his bodily presence was weak, and his speech contemptible" (II Cor. 10:10). However, his convictions could be clearly seen in both his epistles and his conversations.

Such a rebuke had to be an embarrassment to Peter. Why then did Paul handle the problem in this fashion? The answer is simple. Public sins require public criticism and public repentance. Everyone saw what Peter did. There was no way that Paul could have taken Peter aside privately and orally chastised him. Peter deserved this rebuttal "because he was to be blamed." There was sin in his action even though no one but Paul recognized it. Paul interpreted the defection of Peter as a serious violation of the gospel message. The sin had to be stopped immediately.

## B. What Paul Saw in Peter (2:12–13)

Peter's actions were both inconsistent and confusing to others. When he first arrived in Antioch he was having constant

[1]It is stated that the missionaries "abode long time" at Antioch. This would have been a logical time for a visit.

[2]The words "continued" and "some days after" show that there was enough time in which Peter could have paid a visit (Acts 15:35–36).

fellowship with uncircumcised Gentile Christians ("he did eat with the Gentiles").[3] This eating involved participation in the ordinance of the Lord's Supper (I Cor. 11:20–34) and perhaps in the communal meal or love feast which preceded the actual Communion service (II Peter 2:13). This union of Peter with the Gentile believers manifested the oneness in Christ of both Jew and Gentile. This association reinforced the conclusions of the Jerusalem encounter and encouraged the non-Jewish members of the church at Antioch.

However, this communion was quickly replaced by separation. When "certain came from James," the leading elder of the Jerusalem church, Peter's actions and attitudes suddenly changed. The identity of these emissaries is unknown. They were Jewish ("of the circumcision") also, they must have had some delegated authority because they were sent by a key person. Their coming precipitated Peter's two sins: an outward offense and an inward disposition.

### 1. Peter's Defection

Peter "withdrew and separated himself." The force of the two verbs shows that his withdrawal was gradual but steady.[4] At the beginning of the meal, he was with the Gentiles, but at the end, he was sitting only with Jewish Christians. The method of disassociation is not stated. It was probably imperceptible to all, except for Paul. He could see what was going on in Peter's mind through the latter's change in behavior.

This voluntary choice of companions demonstrated the racial prejudice that had marked Peter's life on several occasions. Although Christ had commissioned the apostles to preach to all nations, Peter had not shared the gospel with any Gentile until he was commanded to go to the Roman Cornelius (Acts 10). To this centurion Peter confessed, "Ye know how that it is an unlawful thing for a man that is a Jew to keep company, or come unto one of another nation; but God hath showed me that

[3]The verb "did eat" should be translated "was eating" (sunēsthien). It is in the imperfect tense.

[4]Both verbs are in the imperfect tense.

I should not call any man common or unclean" (Acts 10:28). Up to this point and even beyond, Peter believed in the superiority of the Jewish race over others. This was a proud concept found even within unregenerate Jews.

What compounded the problem was Peter's ignorance of the nature of the true church, the body of Christ. The Corinthians were rebuked for eating and drinking the elements of the Lord's table "unworthily . . . not discerning the Lord's body" (I Cor. 11:29). They failed to manifest the true meaning of Christ's redemptive death but they also exhibited a disunity in the spiritual body of Christ by their divisions. They did not show their oneness in Christ, in whom there is neither rich nor poor, bond nor free, male nor female, and Jew nor Gentile. Peter's departure thus publicly showed the heresy that there were two bodies of Christ or two divisions within the one true church. He made a distinction between Jew and Gentile within Christ.

### 2. Peter's Fear

Actions usually reflect attitudes. The reason why Peter withdrew from the Gentile table was fear ("fearing them which were of the circumcision"). He was afraid of what the Jewish Christians, who were sent from James, might think about his physical identification with Gentile Christians. He probably did not want to lose his testimony before the Jewish members of his home church. In his defection, however, he became an offense to the Gentile believers and actually discredited the truth of racial oneness in Christ.

His actions did not manifest racial prejudice primarily, although the Jewish feeling of superiority was latent within every physical descendant of Abraham. Perhaps the sense of equality had not been fully resolved within Peter's heart and mind. Thus this event simply provided the occasion for that seed of pride to raise its ugly head. Apparently before the ambassadors from James arrived, he fellowshipped with the Gentiles with a clear conscience. After all, he was not the only Jew to do it. The Jewish Christians of the church at Antioch, besides Paul and Barnabas, associated with Peter in this communion.

Earlier in his life, Peter had real personal problems in ministering to Gentiles. He preached to the Roman Cornelius only after God had given him a special vision and then he did it with much mental confusion (Acts 10:9–34). When Cornelius and his family manifested saving faith in Christ by speaking in tongues, both Peter and his Jewish Christian companions were amazed (Acts 10:44–46). When Peter returned to Jerusalem, he was criticized for his missionary endeavor: ". . . they that were of the circumcision contended with him, saying, Thou wentest in to men uncircumcised, and didst eat with them" (Acts 11:2–3). The Jerusalem church then recognized that God planned to save Gentiles as well as Jews (Acts 11:18).

It seems strange that the Peter who boldly preached before the religious leaders was the same man who feared his Jewish friends. Somehow he was afraid of criticism. This sudden visit of those from James must have stimulated the memory of earlier rebuke.

### 3. Peter's Influence (2:13)

It is a scriptural axiom that "none of us liveth to himself, and no man dieth to himself" (Rom. 14:7). Everything that a Christian does affects someone else for benefit or detriment.

Peter's defection had a domino effect upon others. *First,* "the other Jews dissembled likewise with him." The verb "dissembled" (*sunupekrithēsan*) literally means "to commit hypocrisy with." Both Peter and the Jewish Christians became hypocrites. They confessed that they were one with the Gentiles in their spiritual position in Christ, but they denied that truth with their practice of separation. These Jewish Christians who resided in Antioch had to be impressed with the apostolic status of Peter, one of the original followers of Christ. Thus they reasoned that Peter must have been correct when he withdrew from the Gentile table.

*Second,* even Barnabas "also was carried away with their

dissimulation."[5] The associate of Paul was not directly influenced by Peter's action, but when the Jewish Christians, among whom he had labored, departed, he left the Gentile table as well. Thus Peter affected the Jewish Christians who in turn pressured Barnabas.[6]

For living and teaching error, teachers will have a greater accountability and judgment because of their influence on others (James 3:1). Since God had given to Peter a wide area of influence, he needed to weigh more carefully the outcome of his actions. In a real sense, he was morally responsible for the sin of others. When men fall into doctrinal and personal sin, they usually take others with them. Peter should have known better. He started the downfall of the others.

## C. What Paul Said to Peter (2:14)

Rebuke, at times, can be healthy and refreshing. It can help clear the air of misunderstanding and confusion. Solomon wrote that "open rebuke is better than secret love" (Prov. 27:5). He later added: "He that rebuketh a man afterwards shall find more favour than he that flattereth with the tongue" (Prov. 28:23). There is a time to praise and there is a season to rebuke. The situation at Antioch demanded the latter.

### 1. Cause of the Rebuke (2:14a)

The defection of Barnabas was the straw that broke the proverbial camel's back. There is no indication that Paul rebuked Peter immediately after the latter's sin or after the departure of the Jewish segment. It may be, however, that the threefold withdrawal occurred so rapidly that the apostle could not intervene. It may be that Paul waited for Barnabas to deal

[5]The words "dissembled" and "dissimulation" both come from the Greek word for "hypocrisy."

[6]The presence of Barnabas with Paul in Antioch is another argument for the view that the epistle was written sometime before the second journey. Paul and Barnabas separated at the start of the second trip (Acts 15:36-41).

with the defectors; instead, the associate joined the sinning Christians.

Paul "saw that they walked not uprightly according to the truth of the gospel." Their feet literally did not walk in a straight line (*orthopodousi*). They staggered or wavered like a drunkard who is asked to walk a straight line in a DWI (driving while intoxicated) test. The standard or goal which they violated was "the truth of the gospel." The gospel message saved Jews and Gentiles alike. Christ "is our peace, who hath made both one, and hath broken down the middle wall of partition between us" (Eph. 2:14).

### 2. Content of the Rebuke (2:14b)

Paul openly criticized Peter "before them all." He condemned neither Barnabas nor the Jewish Christians directly; however, they were also implicated because of their involvement in Peter's hypocrisy. The rebuke was directly aimed at Peter because he was the instigator of the problem. He started the separation and he could produce the reconciliation. Since this was a public sin against the Gentile members, Paul had to confront Peter publicly. The issue had to be settled in an open forum.

*First,* Paul described Peter's spiritual practice before the defection. Peter was a Jew, yet he lived "after the manner of Gentiles, and not as do the Jews."[7] Peter did not obey the law to gain or to keep salvation. He did not follow the requirements of the Judaizers or of the religious elders, composed of the Pharisees and the priests. This was the exact status of Gentile believers.

*Second,* he raised the question: "Why compellest thou the Gentiles to live as do the Jews?" Peter actually expected more of the Gentiles than he did of himself. In a sense, he reflected the sin of the scribes and Pharisees: "For they bind heavy burdens and grievous to be borne, and lay them on men's shoulders; but they themselves will not move them with one of their

[7]The conditional particle "if" (*ei*) introduces a statement true to life. Peter *was* living like a Gentile.

fingers" (Matt. 23:4). Peter resisted the pressure of the Judaizers to force Titus to be circumcised but now he acted as if he wanted the Gentile believers to Judaize. His defection could have been used as an argument that the Gentiles were not really saved or that they were inferior Christians.

## II. EXPLANATION OF DIVINE JUSTIFICATION (2:15–21)

Did Paul state this next section of seven verses (2:15–21) to Peter? Does it represent the gist of the apostolic rebuke? It is difficult to determine with certainty the answers to those questions. Regardless, this section serves as a fitting transition from the autobiographical argument for Paul's apostolic ministry (chs. 1–2) to the theological argument for justification by faith (chs. 3–4). It also forms a definite link between the criticism of Peter and his associates (2:14) and the rebuke of the "foolish Galatians" (3:1).

### A. Definition of Justification (2:15–16)

Job theorized, "How should man be just with God?" (Job 9:2). On the other side, how could God remain just and justify any sinner? The principles of civil and spiritual justice are the same: "If there be a controversy between men, and they come unto judgment, that the judges may judge them; then they shall justify the righteous, and condemn the wicked" (Deut. 25:1). When an innocent man is jailed or a guilty person is acquitted, that action is a miscarriage of justice and an abomination to the Lord (Prov. 17:15).

To *justify* means to "declare righteous." The role of the judge is to declare righteous that person who is already righteous. Since "there is none righteous, no, not one" (Rom. 3:10), how could any man be justified by a holy God?

#### 1. Its Necessity (2:15)

Before God there is a difference in human morality. The "Jews by nature" were not as subject to the vices of the Gentiles because of the civil, ceremonial, and moral restraints of the Mosaic law. They believed in one holy God who had spoken authoritatively in the Old Testament. A permissive society could not function within the theocracy of Israel.

On the other hand, the "sinners of the Gentiles" had not been restricted by positive and negative commandments. Their behavior reflected a pagan, polytheistic culture devoid of public morality.

Although their outward practice differed, both Jews and Gentiles shared the same spiritual position before God. They were equally "under sin" (Rom. 3:9). They were under the penalty of sin, controlled by the power of sin, and limited by a mortal, corruptible body. Paul observed, "For as many as have sinned without law shall also perish without law: and as many as have sinned in the law shall be judged by the law" (Rom. 2:12).

The total depravity of the human race before a righteous God means that all men are as *bad off* as they can be (position), not that they are as *bad* as they can be (practice). They are all guilty, lost sinners, unable to do anything that will change their spiritual standing. They stand condemned. If they are to be declared righteous, they must be first made righteous.

### 2. Its Means (2:16)

*Negatively,* justification is not "by the works of the law." Paul emphasized this negation three times within this verse. There is nothing wrong with the law; it is holy, just, and good (Rom. 7:12). The problem lies within the spiritual impotence of sinful man (Rom. 8:3). God never gave the law so that sinners might try to obey it in order to gain eternal life (3:21). No person, unaided by the Spirit of God, can do any good, righteous deed that will bring to him the righteousness of God (Rom. 3:10, 12). The apostle was firm in the conviction that "by the works of the law shall no flesh be justified" (2:16; cf. Rom. 3:20).

*Positively,* justification is "by the faith of Jesus Christ." He stressed this assertion three times in this verse.[8] This faith is in the person and the redemptive work of Christ. In His sacrificial death He provided redemption from sin, reconciliation for the world, and the propitiation of God's just requirements. This gracious provision, however, must be appropriated by simple trust. When a sinner puts his total dependence in the Savior, then he receives a righteous standing before God. He is made righteous *in Christ* (I Cor. 1:30; II Cor. 5:21; Phil. 3:7–9).

After the imputation of the righteousness of God to the believing sinner, he can now be declared righteous by God. Thus justification is the act of God whereby He declares righteous that sinner who has been made righteous through faith in Christ (Rom. 4:5; 23–25). The doctrine of justification is described in seven ways: (1) its source is God (Rom. 3:26; 8:30); (2) its essence is grace (Rom. 3:24); (3) its means is faith (Rom. 5:1); (4) its ground is the blood of Christ (Rom. 5:9); (5) its position is in Christ (I Cor. 6:11); (6) its divine agent is the Holy Spirit (I Cor. 6:11); and (7) its evidence is works (James 2:21, 24).

Before imputation and justification, the sinner was as *bad off* as he could possibly be. After those divine acts have changed his spiritual standing, he is now as *good off* as he can be. He has been made "accepted in the beloved" Son of God (Eph. 1:6).

This is why Paul "believed in Jesus Christ." He later testified, ". . . that I may win Christ, and be found in him, not having mine own righteousness, which is of the law, but that which is through the faith of Christ, the righteousness which is of God by faith" (Phil. 3:8–9).

## B. Defense of Justification (2:17–21)

### 1. Relationship to the Law (2:17–19)

Paul then assumed a hypothetical situation to be true in order that he might prove a theological point ("But if . . . we ourselves are found sinners"). The Judaizers claimed that the

[8]The words "of Jesus Christ" must be seen as an objective genitive. He becomes the object of the sinner's faith.

uncircumcised Gentiles who accepted justification by faith in Christ alone were still unsaved. Paul, circumcised as a Jewish infant, put his trust in the Savior in order to be justified by faith alone; thus he repudiated the meritorious value of his initiatory rite. In the opinion of the Judaizers, Paul like the Gentiles was also an unregenerate sinner because of his actions.

The logic of the Judaizers would make Christ into "the minister of sin." This is a ridiculous conclusion. How could the sinless Son of God encourage any person to commit sin through a total dependence upon Him? "God forbid!"

The charge of sinfulness against Paul actually came during the time of his past conversion life ("while we seek to be justified by Christ"). As long as he tried to establish his own righteousness, he was thoroughly acceptable to the legalistic Jews (cf. Rom. 10:3). He was "blameless" in his attempt to gain righteousness through the law (Phil. 3:6). He tried to be moral, to be good. When he believed in Christ, however, he eliminated all of that human effort. Although he no longer tried to obey the law as a means of salvation, he still wanted to please Christ through total submission to Him. Christ could not be accused as being the author of sin simply because a person stopped his endeavor to obey the Mosaic law.

If Paul had yielded to the pressure to have Titus circumcised or if he had not questioned Peter's defection, he would have rebuilt the system of legal righteousness ("for if I build again the things which I destroyed"). In his pharisaical life, he had established for himself the basis of divine acceptance through his religious achievements (1:13–14; Phil. 3:4–6). After his conversion and reception of divine revelation, he preached that the keeping of the Mosaic law could not justify anyone (Acts 13:39). In fact, he "destroyed" the system of legalism. Now the Judaizers wanted him to denounce justification by faith alone and to "build again" the old religion of works.

To do so Paul would have made himself a "transgressor." In one sense, he would have sinned against the law by abandoning it as the means of salvation; in another, he would have offended the principle of grace by requiring human effort.

Although the keeping of the law is not necessary to gain salvation, it is essential to prepare men to receive the right-eousness of God by faith (2:19). Paul wrote, "the law is good, if a man use it lawfully" (I Tim. 1:8). By attempting to obey the law ("through the law"), he actually "died [*apethanon*] to the law." Elsewhere, he explained:

> But sin, taking occasion by the commandment, wrought in me all manner of concupiscence. For without the law sin was dead. For I was alive without the law once: but when the com-mandment came, sin revived, and *I died*. And the command-ment, which was ordained to life, I found to be *unto death*. For sin, taking occasion by the commandment, deceived me, and by it slew me. Wherefore the law is holy, and the commandment holy, and just and good. Was then that which is good *made death* unto me? God forbid. But sin, that it might appear sin, *working death* in me by that which is good; that sin by the commandment might become exceeding sinful (Rom. 7:8-13, emphasis mine).

The law killed him by demonstrating that he had broken the law, that he was sinful, and that he stood guilty before God. The law had served its divine purpose by preparing him to accept God's gracious provision of redemption. Through death to human effort he could become alive through faith ("that I might live unto God"). In Christ the believer is dead to the law (Rom. 7:4, 6). He is under no obligation to keep it as the means of justification or sanctification.

### 2. *Justification with Christ (2:20)*

The justified standing of the believer has five characteris-tics. *First,* the Christian has been "crucified with Christ." When Jesus Christ died on the cross the believer was spiritu-ally crucified with Him. God saw the believer in Christ, co-crucified. Positionally the child of God died in Him, rose in Him, ascended in Him, and is seated in Him in heaven (Rom. 6:3-5; Eph. 2:1-6). In Christ he died to the penalty of a broken law because the Savior bore the wrath as his substitute.

*Second,* the believer is alive spiritually ("nevertheless I live"). Christ came to give life (John 10:10). The believing sinner has been quickened in order that he might be joined to Christ in an eternal union (Rom. 7:4, 6).

*Third,* the believer has life because Christ lives in him ("Christ liveth in me"). On the night before His crucifixion, Christ said to His own, "At that day ye shall know that I am in my Father, and ye in me, and I in you" (John 14:20). The mystery of redemption is "Christ in you, the hope of glory" (Col. 1:27).

*Fourth,* the justified life is a faith life ("I live by the faith of the Son of God"). Saving faith is that act of the sinner whereby he initially puts his total trust in the Savior's gracious person and sacrificial death and continues to leave it there throughout his lifetime. Justification begins and ends with faith. It is "revealed from faith to faith: as it is written, The just shall live by faith" (Rom. 1:17).

*Fifth,* it is a life made possible by Christ's love and death ("who loved me, and gave himself for me"). The justified person recognizes that Christ loved him personally ("me") and that He was his vicarious substitute.

### 3. Incompatible with Legalism (2:21)

In conclusion, Paul pointed out that justification by works only or by faith and works is diametrically opposed to justification by grace through faith. Later he will show that the concept of faith and works is really just a works principle (4:19–31). The heresy of the Judaizers discredited the divine program of redemption in two ways.

*First,* it "frustrates the grace of God." If a man can earn salvation, then God must give him what he deserves. However, the essence of grace is for God to give men what they do not deserve. Elsewhere Paul argued, "Now to him that worketh is the reward not reckoned of grace, but of debt" (Rom. 4:4). A works salvation nullifies the grace principle (Eph. 2:8–9).

*Second,* it deprecates the cross of Christ ("then Christ is dead in vain"). He died unnecessarily if a man can gain the righteousness of God through legal obedience. The issue is clear: Did Jesus Christ completely satisfy the righteous demands of God on the cross? What did He mean when He said,

"It is finished" (John 19:30). If man must add to what He did, Christ should have declared that it was partially finished. If men can gain or keep a justified standing by works, then they are implying that Christ provided an incomplete atonement. Such people must answer the question, How much did Christ do and how much must they do?

## QUESTIONS FOR DISCUSSION

1. For what reasons should believers be publicly rebuked? By whom? Are people afraid to take this drastic action? Why?
2. Of whom are Christians more afraid? Of believers? Of the unsaved? Why?
3. Do Christians show partiality within the local church? Can the Jewish-Gentile controversy be equated with the black-white integration problem?
4. In what ways can Christians cause others to follow them in their sins? Can anything be done to eliminate this type of influence?
5. Is legalism a problem today? In what ways do groups force works upon their people as a basis for justification and sanctification?
6. Do believers manifest the truth that Christ is living in them? What prevents this public show of spiritual life?
7. Is there a lack of theological preaching and teaching today? What can be done to improve the situation?

# 5

## The Examination of True Spiritual Experience
*Galatians 3:1–9*

The Bible alone must be the basis of faith and practice. The dogmatic pronouncements of impressive preachers should never be substituted for the clear exposition of God's Word. Long ago Isaiah warned, "To the law and to the testimony: if they speak not according to this word, it is because there is no light in them" (Isa. 8:20).

Genuine experience, consequently, should issue from a humble response to the written revelation of God. Paul now wanted the Galatians to examine their convictions and experiences in the light of his ministry in their midst. He wanted them to compare their spiritual achievement by what he taught and by what the Judaizers proclaimed. He also desired them to relate their reception of justification with that of Abraham.

### I. IN THE LIVES OF THE GALATIANS (3:1-5)

The believers at Galatia were last addressed personally much earlier in the book (1:2, 11). Now, a sharp characterization is leveled at them (3:1, 3). In a series of six questions within these five verses, Paul tried to get them to rethink their initial contact with the gospel message. They had quickly forgotten what had happened to them.

## A. Their Problem (3:1)

### 1. They Were Foolish

These words must have really hurt their souls: "O foolish Galatians." No one wants to be called a fool, let alone publicly and by a friend. Yet Paul did it twice (3:1, 3). The adjective "foolish" (*anoētoi*) literally means "no understanding," thought, or perception. They had intelligence, but they did not use it properly in their quick acceptance of heresy. This is the same word that Jesus Christ used to chastise the two disciples on the road to Emmaus after His resurrection: "O fools, and slow of heart to believe all that the prophets have spoken" (Luke 24:25). These two were despondent because they had not properly correlated the prophecies about Christ's sufferings and His subsequent glory (Luke 24:26–27). Just as Christ needed to explain the Old Testament Scriptures to them, so Paul had to exegete the divine plan of redemption for the Galatians. The cure for spiritual foolishness is biblical understanding.

In his critical rebuke the apostle did not violate the warning of the Lord: " . . . whosoever shall say, Thou fool, shall be in danger of hell fire" (Matt. 5:22). This is a different word for "fool" (*more*). The English term *moron* is based on this Greek word. When a person hates his enemy with intense anger, he is very likely to use this contemptible title.

Paul, however, loved the Galatians, his spiritual brethren. Through his shocking description and the series of six questions, he wanted to shake them out of their spiritual and mental doldrums. An Arabian proverb states, "He who knows and knows not that he knows: he is asleep; wake him!" The Galatians needed to wake up and to be alert to the doctrinal dangers around them.

It is not wrong to be ignorant if that lack of knowledge stems from immaturity. For example, a first grade student cannot be expected to know the principles of algebra. The Galatian foolishness, however, reflected a gullible stupidity. They should have known better. They actually received the same rebuke that the apostle had given to other churches. To the

Corinthians he said six times, "Know ye not . . .?" (I Cor. 6:2, 3, 9, 15, 16, 19). To the Thessalonians he declared, "But I would not have you to be ignorant" (I Thess. 4:13). The Galatians thus needed to proceed from a lack of understanding to a practical discernment of their problem.

## 2. They Were Bewitched

Paul's question was direct: "Who hath bewitched you?" The singular interrogative pronoun "who" (*tis*) indicates that the ringleader of the heretical group had hoodwinked them (cf. 1:9; 5:10). The verb "bewitched" (*ebaskane*) means to bring evil on someone by an evil eye or by hypocritical praise or to lead astray by evil deeds. In a sense, the Galatians were victims of an evil spell. They must have been hypotized or awe struck by the forceful oratory of the key Judaizer.

The result of their spiritual bewilderment was disobedience to the truth of justification by faith ("that ye should not obey the truth"). The issue was clear: the Judaizers claimed that the Gentile Christians would remain disobedient if they did not submit to the necessity of circumcision for salvation. On the other hand, the apostle reacted that they would become disobedient by any attempt to use legalism as a means of redemption.

When Paul had originally evangelized the region of Galatia he simply set forth the truth of Christ's crucifixion and resurrection ("before whose eyes Jesus Christ hath been evidently set forth, crucified among you"). In fact, the apostle so vividly portrayed the historic, objective details of the Cross that the Galatians received a mental picture of that event. It was just as real to them as if they had been standing at the foot of Golgotha. The verb "evidently set forth" means "to write before" (*proegraphē*). It was used of posters, placards, or public proclamations placed on walls so that people could see and read them clearly. Both the facts and the significance of the crucifixion were forthrightly presented. The Galatians knew exactly why Christ died before they exercised faith in Him. With understanding quickened by the Holy Spirit, they trusted Him who had accomplished a finished atonement.

## B. His Solution (3:2-5)

The next four verses contain five questions. By analyzing the ramifications of their answers, the Galatians would be able to discover for themselves that Paul was right and that the Judaizers were wrong.

### 1. How Did You Receive the Spirit? (3:2)

Although he regarded them as "foolish," he wanted to learn something from them ("This only would I learn of you"). Paul was willing for himself to be the student and for them to be the teacher.

In this exchange of roles he asked them, "Received ye the Spirit by the works of the law, or by the hearing of faith?" The past tense verb ("received") points to the time of their conversion and shows that the apostle accepted them as genuine believers. He did not doubt that the Holy Spirit had come to indwell them; he simply wanted them to tell him *how* they received the Spirit. He gave them a choice of two divergent answers. The means was either "works" or "faith." There is no hint that they could have received the Spirit by faith and works. The usage of the definite article ("*the* Spirit") emphasizes the reference to the person of the Holy Spirit rather than to His gifts.

If the Judaizers had been correct, then it would have been impossible for the uncircumcized Gentile converts to have received the Spirit at all. Yet the Galatians "were filled with joy, and with the Holy Spirit" as the result of Paul's evangelistic efforts (Acts 13:52). To accept the heresy of the Judaizers would be to deny the presence of the Spirit in their lives. Would they be ready to make such an admission?

The Holy Spirit indwells the believer at the very moment of saving faith ("hearing of faith"). This phrase does not refer to a postconversion experience. The faith that brings justification also brings the indwelling presence of the Spirit. It takes place at regeneration when a sinner is born into the family of God (John 1:12). He later wrote, "And because ye are sons, God hath sent forth the Spirit of his Son into your hearts, crying, Abba, Father" (4:6). In the normal pattern of this age, there is no such group as Christians who do not have the Spirit. Paul firmly stated, "Now if any man have not the Spirit of Christ, he is none of his" (Rom. 8:9).

No man has believed apart from the hearing of the Word of God (Rom. 10:17). They heard Paul preach and they believed. They were then sealed with the Spirit until the day of redemption (Eph. 1:13).

## 2. How Will You Be Made Perfect? (3:3)

Paul knew what their answer would be (3:2). Of course they would reply that they had received the Spirit when he evangelized them. That expectation prompted the apostle to raise his next question: "Are ye so foolish?"[1] He was baffled by their apparent immature acceptance of the heresy. They just did not utilize the laws of logic and common sense.

Are the means of justification and sanctification different or the same? He asked them whether they planned to change the method by which they had found acceptance with God. Did they plan to start in one way, but to finish with another? He probed further into their spiritual consciousness: "Having begun in the Spirit, are ye now made perfect by the flesh?" The opening participle ("having begun") shows that they had made a proper, biblical start.[2] The Holy Spirit had convicted them of sin, righteousness, and judgment (John 16:8–11). They had been filled with the Spirit and had produced the fruit of the Spirit (5:22; cf. Acts 13:52). All of these glorious realities were manifested in their early Christian experience long before the Judaizers entered their territory.

In what ways were they trying to be "made perfect by the flesh"? The Judaizers wanted them to be circumcised (5:2), to observe a ritualistic calendar (4:10), and to keep the Mosaic law (6:13). To them justification by faith was a start in the

[1]The emphasis in the Greek reads this way: "So foolish are ye?"

[2]The participle (enarxamenoi) is in the aorist tense. This points to their completed conversion experience.

right direction, but it had to end up with justification by the law (3:11; 5:4). What seemed logical to the heretics was foolish to the apostle. In one sense, the position of the Judaizers can be compared with the baking of a cake. According to them, you first put it into an oven; then you take it out and finish it by placing it in a refrigerator. Both heat and cold will not produce a cake, and neither will faith and works produce justification.

In the gospel message "is the righteousness of God revealed from faith to faith: as it is written. The just shall live by faith" (Rom. 1:17). Faith is both the source ("from," *ek*) and the goal ("to," *eis*) of justification. A sinner receives the righteousness of God by faith and he manifests his justified standing by a life of faith. Thus he begins and ends with the same means: faith. A man is both justified and sanctified by faith.

### 3. Why Did You Suffer? (3:4)

At the end of the first missionary journey Paul and Barnabas retraced their steps and ministered again to the Galatian converts: "Confirming the souls of the disciples, and exhorting them to continue in the faith, and that we must through much tribulation enter into the kingdom of God" (Acts 14:21–22). Both the apostles and the new Christians had experienced persecution in that region. At Antioch in Pisidia there was verbal abuse and a forced expulsion (Acts 13:44–45, 50); however the Galatian "disciples were filled with joy, and with the Holy Spirit" (Acts 13:52). At Iconium the believers tasted mental hatred and physical threats (Acts 14:2, 5). At Lystra Paul was so severely stoned that he was dragged out of the city as a dead man (Acts 14:19).

Thus this question was most appropriate: "Have ye suffered so many things in vain?" If they were still unsaved, as the Judaizers claimed, why did the unbelieving Jews and Gentiles persecute them? According to Christ, the world loves its own (John 15:19). The real reason why the unregenerate hated them, persecuted them, kicked them out of the synagogue, and even attempted to kill them is because they saw the presence of Christ within the lives of the believers (John 15:18—16:2). If they were still unsaved because they had not accepted legalistic circumcision, then they suffered needlessly.

Paul knew, though, that their suffering had genuine spiritual cause and purpose. They were saved under his ministry and they would not defect to the Judaizers once they knew the facts. His assurance is indicated in the phrase: ". . . if it be yet in vain."[3] It wasn't, and he did not expect that it would be.

They had experienced both outward tribulation and inward joy (John 16:33). This was a definite sign of true repentance and faith (II Thess. 1:4–5).

### 4. How Did God Perform Miracles? (3:5)

Two supernatural acts had been done in Galatia. *First,* God had imparted the Holy Spirit to the believers ("He therefore that ministereth to you the Spirit"); and *second,* He had performed miracles in their midst ("and worketh miracles among you"). The *fact* of these divine operations could not be questioned; the *means,* however, was the issue. Were they done "by the works of the law, or by the hearing of faith"? These were the only two possible options (cf. 3:2). In no way could they have occurred by faith *and* works.

The historical background, recorded in the Book of Acts, again provides the answer to this final question. When Paul and Barnabas were at Iconium: "Long time therefore abode they speaking boldly in the Lord, which gave testimony unto the word of his grace, and granted signs and wonders to be done by their hands" (Acts 14:3). Later at Lystra Paul healed a man who had been a cripple since birth (Acts 14:8–11). The pagans responded to the miracle by ascribing deity to the apostle. Subsequently Paul was stoned, leaving him either dead or in a death-like coma; but he was miraculously raised up (Acts 14:19–20). The Galatians were the beneficiaries of the divine operation within Paul, authenticating him to be a genuine apostle with the true message. Paul could also say to them, "Truly the signs of an apostle were wrought among you in all

---

[3]There is a difference in the words translated as "vain" (*dōrean*; 2:21, cf. *eikē*; 3:4, twice).

patience, in signs, and wonders, and mighty deeds" (II Cor. 12:12). The Greek term for "mighty deeds" (*dunameis*) is the same as that translated as "miracles" (3:5). This supernatural display was produced by the preaching of the simple gospel of justification by faith. At no time was the necessity of legal works introduced.

The verb "ministereth" (*epichorēgōn*) shows that the Galatians received the person of the Holy Spirit and all of the attendant gifts and blessings connected with the Spirit during Paul's ministry. The word was used of a benefactor of the chorus at a pagan festival who would supply the costumes and the cost of training. Thus there was nothing more of the Spirit that the Galatians could get through the Judaizers. In fact, the false teachers had contributed nothing that was spiritual or miraculous.

## II. IN THE LIFE OF ABRAHAM (3:6-9)

In these two chapters, the name of Abraham will be mentioned nine times (3:6, 7, 8, 9, 14, 16, 18, 29; 4:22). But why is he so important? Why was not some other prominent Old Testament character selected? Two reasons are suggested. The *first* is that Abraham became the father of the Jewish people when God established an unconditional covenant with him (Gen. 12:1-3; 13:14-18; 15:1-21; 17:1-8). From that historic event, God identified Himself to Israel as the God of Abraham, Isaac, and Jacob. The *second* is that the first mention of faith and imputed righteousness is attributed to Abraham (Gen. 15:6).

Thus the issue of Abraham's justification is very relevant. How was he saved? Did he exercise faith only, or did he have to be circumcised in order to inherit the divine blessing?

### A. Necessity of Faith Alone (3:6-7)

The spiritual experience of Abraham provided a pattern for all of his physical and spiritual posterity. The usage of the connective "even as" (*kathōs*) indicates that the justification of Abraham became the standard for both Jews and Gentiles. A Jew who traced his racial and religious heritage to the patriarch had to be justified in the same way as his ancestral father. Although the Gentile could not trace his physical roots to Abraham, nevertheless he also had to be declared righteous in similar fashion because the universal blessings of the Abrahamic covenant applied to him (cf. 3:8). In addition, the connective *even as* joins the experiences of the Galatians to that of Abraham (cf. 3:1–5).

### 1. For Abraham (3:6)

How was he justified? The answer is simple, yet pointed: "Abraham believed God, and it was accounted to him for righteousness." This statement is a direct quotation of the first reference to faith in the Old Testament (Gen. 15:6; cf. Rom. 4:3). Four facts about his faith must be seen. *First,* the *object* of his faith was "God," not himself nor a rite. What gives value to faith is the object of that belief. One wrote, "But without faith it is impossible to please him: for he that cometh to God must believe that he is, and that he is a rewarder of them that diligently seek him" (Heb. 11:6). He did not believe something about God; rather he "believed God."

*Second,* the *content* of his faith was the helplessness of self and the ability of God to perform what He promised. God told the patriarch that his descendants would be as the sand of the sea and as the stars of the sky (Gen. 15:5). At that time both Abraham and Sarah were elderly, and Sarah had a history of barrenness. The situation looked impossible, yet Abraham trusted God.

> Who against hope believed in hope, that he might become the father of many nations; according to that which was spoken, So shall thy seed be. And being not weak in faith, he considered not his own body now dead, when he was about an hundred years old, neither yet the deadness of Sarah's womb: He staggered not at the promise of God through unbelief: but was strong in faith, giving glory to God; and being fully persuaded that, what he had

promised, he was able also to perform. And therefore it was imputed to him for righteousness (Rom. 4:18–22).

*Third,* the *time* of his faith was before he was circumcised (Gen. 15:6; cf. Gen. 17:9–27). The Judaizers argued that since Abraham believed and was circumcised, the Galatians would also have to be circumcised in order to receive the righteousness of God. However, a righteous standing was imputed to the patriarch at the moment of faith. The argument is decisive: If circumcision is necessary for salvation, then why did God give His righteousness to the patriarch before he submitted to the rite? A man is not justified before he is saved. Elsewhere Paul debated:

> How was it then reckoned? When he was in circumcision, or in uncircumcision? Not in circumcision, but in uncircumcision. And he received the sign of circumcision, a seal of the righteousness of the faith which he had yet being uncircumcised: that he might be the father of all them that believe, though they be not circumcised, that righteousness might be imputed unto them also (Rom. 4:10–11).

Circumcision, thus, was an evidence of justification, not a requirement for it.

*Fourth,* the *result* of his faith was the reception of the imputed righteousness of God. It "was accounted" (*elogisthē*) to him. In the divine ledger his debt of sin was forgiven, paid completely by the redemptive death of Christ. In addition, God deposited His righteousness into the account of Abraham. The patriarch, in his spiritual standing, was now "holy and without blame before him in love" (Eph. 1:4).

### 2. For His Children (3:7)

The Galatians, who did not use their intelligence to perceive the error of the Judaizers, are now commanded to employ their minds in the understanding of a logical conclusion ("Know ye therefore").

All who seek justification by faith ("they which are of faith") are really the spiritual "children of Abraham." This classification includes both regenerated Jews and Gentiles (Rom. 4:13–16).

Jews are the physical children of Abraham, but that fact alone does not make them the *true* children of Abraham. When Paul was in Galatia, he addressed his synagogue listeners like this: "Men and brethren, children of the stock of Abraham, and whosoever among you that feareth God [Gentile circumcised proselytes], to you is the word of this salvation sent" (Acts 13:26). He recognized their racial identity but he also knew that they were unsaved. Paul even admitted that the Judaizers were the seed of Abraham but he also characterized them as satanic ministers (II Cor. 11:13–15; cf. 11:22).

John the Baptist charged the religious leaders of his day not to put their confidence in their physical lineage (Matt. 3:9). To the same crowd Jesus declared, "If ye were Abraham's children, ye would do the works of Abraham" (John 8:39).

Paul further explained, "For they are not all Israel which are of Israel: Neither, because they are the seed of Abraham, are they all children" (Rom. 9:6–7). The growth of the Jewish nation went from Abraham to Isaac to Jacob. Abraham had other sons born to Hagar and to Keturah, but the national covenant promises did not extend to them. Esau, the twin of Jacob, also was excluded from the covenant blessings. The real child of Abraham within Israel is that person who has been justified by faith. In addition, the Gentile who has been declared righteous by faith can also be called a child of Abraham. The determining factor, therefore, is spiritual identification, not physical connection.

## B. Blessing of the Covenant (3:8–9)

The authority for these declarations is "the scripture" (3:8). The usage of the singular shows that although the Bible is composed of sixty-six books written by about forty men, it really is one book authored by God. The unique expression ("the scripture . . . preached") means that God and the Bible must be equated (cf. II Tim. 3:16). Thus "God says" and "the Bible says" are identical. The spiritual Christian therefore manifests his submission to God by his obedience to the written Word of God.

## 1. For All Peoples Potentially (3:8)

The Abrahamic covenant was a prophetic anticipation of the means by which "God would justify the heathen [Gentile nations]."[4] The present justification of the uncircumcised Galatians was actually foreseen in the universal aspects of the covenant promises ("foreseeing"). The means was "through faith" (literally "out of faith;" *ek pisteōs*).[5]

The actual covenant blessings, spoken by God directly to Abraham, are equated with the verbal phrase: ". . . preached the gospel" (*proeuēggelisato*). The "gospel" is always the message that God has graciously provided spiritual blessings and that these favors can only be received by faith.[6] Abraham believed that proclamation, received the imputed righteousness of God, and was justified. The fact that he heard before he was circumcised and before the Mosaic law was instituted demonstrated that all of the world's population must be saved according to his human example. Again, God does not have two ways of salvation: one for the circumcised Jew and another for the uncircumcised Gentile. Both must approach God through the spiritual provision of the Abrahamic covenant.

The universal aspects of that great promise are seen in the prediction: "In thee shall all nations be blessed" (cf. Gen. 12:3). Some of the covenant promises were personal in nature: "I will bless thee, and make thy name great" (Gen. 12:2). Others pertained to the nation of Israel: "I will make of thee a great nation" (Gen. 12:2). However, the phrase "all nations" includes all peoples, both Jewish and Gentile.

## 2. For All Believers Specifically (3:9)

Just as all Jews do not qualify to be known as the children of Abraham (3:7), so all nations will not automatically receive the

---

[4]Literally it reads: ". . . that God is justifying the nations out of faith."

[5]The same preposition *ek* is used here as elsewhere ("by," 3:2; "of," 3:7).

[6]The word *gospel* means "good message or news" (*eu,* "good" and *aggelion,* "message").

universal blessings of the covenant. There is a difference between provision and appropriation. The blessing only comes to "they which be of faith." The Bible does not teach universalism, the concept that all men will eventually be saved.

Just as the patriarch personally expressed belief in order to receive the righteousness of God in his day ("faithful Abraham"),[7] so both the Jew and the Gentile must only trust God in the same way to receive the same righteousness. There is no difference in the way that Abraham was justified and the means by which all subsequent generations have been declared righteous.

## QUESTIONS FOR DISCUSSION

1. In what ways are modern Christians bewitched by false teachers? Why don't they use their spiritual intelligence? What can be done to correct the problem?
2. Do evangelical preachers clearly preach the significance of the crucifixion? Are the physical sufferings of Christ emphasized more than His spiritual torment?
3. Why are believers ignorant about the time and the purpose of the reception of the Holy Spirit?
4. What groups stress salvation by faith and works? If people believe that baptism is essential for salvation, are they any different than the unsaved Judaizers?
5. Did God save men in a different way in past ages? Why do some evangelicals teach that men were saved by legalism in the Old Testament?
6. Are the heathen lost? Can they be saved in any other way besides the hearing of the gospel?
7. Are Christians ignorant of the Old Testament? Its theology? Its relationship to the New Testament? What can be done to improve this situation?

[7]The adjective "faithful" shows that he had an active faith. He was a constant believer. At no time did he add works in order to gain or maintain his justified standing.

# 6

## *The Relationships of the Law*
### *Galatians 3:10–18*

The subject of the law was introduced earlier in the second chapter (2:16). It subsequently becomes a major theme in the book, being mentioned twenty-nine times in the last five chapters.[1]

The designation "law" is used in several ways. *First,* it can refer to the entire Old Testament canon of thirty-nine books (John 10:34). *Second,* it can point specifically to the first five books written by Moses. In this usage it is set in contrast with the other general sections of the Old Testament, called either "the prophets" (Matt. 5:17; Luke 24:27) or "the prophets and the psalms" (Luke 24:44). *Third,* it can include only the moral, civil, and ceremonial regulations given to Israel at Mount Sinai (Heb. 9:19). *Fourth,* it can restrict itself to the Ten Commandments (Matt. 22:36–40). It is difficult to determine how the New Testament authors used it in every passage; regardless, it always pointed to the basis of Jewish faith and practice. The issue was whether conformity to the system of legalism was necessary for salvation. Paul was against such legalism in any form because it was diametrically opposed to the principle of grace: "For the law was given by Moses, but grace and truth came by Jesus Christ" (John 1:17).

In this passage, the apostle will discuss the relationships of

---

[1]Excluding Romans, there are more references to the law in Galatians than in all of Paul's other epistles combined.

the law to both the curse of God and the covenant of God made with Abraham.

## I. THE LAW AND THE CURSE (3:10-14)

The connective "for" (*gar*) joins this section to the preceding two. Both the Galatians and Abraham had experiences of justification by faith "for" it was impossible for them to have gained the righteousness of God by legalistic works.

Earlier Paul proved that a man could not be justified by the works of the law (2:16), that he could not receive the Holy Spirit by legalism (3:2), and that he could not perform miracles by those same works (3:5). What then could the law do? It could put a man under its curse. This was its dilemma.

### A. Dilemma of the Law (3:10-12)

#### 1. The Law Can Curse (3:10)

All men are "under sin" (Rom. 3:9). They are totally depraved. In their position before God, they are as bad off as they can be. They are condemned, destined for perdition, unless they are redeemed.

In addition, sinful men are "under the curse." This is a special curse that pertains to "as many as are of the works of the law." This group seeks to be justified by human effort through legal obedience. They are just the opposite of the group named "they which be of faith" (3:9). The legalism crowd is firmly committed to the proposition that a man can gain divine favor by compliance to a system of moral regulations. Such people are deeply convinced that they have the ability within themselves to do what God commands. If pressed, they may admit that they are not perfect and that they occasionally break the spiritual law of God, but they believe that they have done sufficiently enough good deeds for which they will be eternally rewarded.

Partial or temporary obedience, however, is not adequate. Both God and the law demanded perfect obedience of all of the law all of the time. In support of this axiom, Paul quoted the authoritative conclusion to the list of curses imposed upon Israel: "Cursed is everyone that continueth not in all things which are written in the book of the law to do them" (cf. Deut. 27: 26). To escape the curse of a broken law one must know all that God has commanded; consequently ignorance of any precept can never be accepted as a valid excuse. To escape one must obey all of the divine directives; therefore, 99 percent obedience is still reckoned to be failure. To escape one must keep the law continually; thus one error at the end of a life completely overshadows the obedience of a lifetime.

On the other hand, to fall under the curse a person needs only to break *one* commandment *once*. To gain the title *criminal* in modern society, a person does not have to violate all of the written laws. He only needs to rob one bank once or to murder one human being once. To be known as a cursed sinner he only has to break one of the Ten Commandments once. Of course, no person outside of Jesus Christ has ever kept all of the law all of the time.

In fact, Christ asserted that the violation of moral law occurred not only in the outward action, but also in the inward attitude. He explained:

> Ye have heard that it was said by them of old time, Thou shalt not commit adultery: But I say unto you, that whosoever looketh on a woman to lust after her hath committed adultery with her already in his heart (Matt. 5:27-28).

A person can sin in thought and intent as well as in deed.

On one occasion Jesus Christ challenged the rich young ruler to keep the commandments contained in the second table (Matt. 19:16-19). The wealthy man reacted: "All these things have I kept from my youth up: what lack I yet?" (Matt. 19:20). This aristrocrat personified those who are "of the works of the law." They think that they have been obedient, but they actually have disobeyed. To reveal to the ruler that he actually loved himself and his riches more than his neighbor, Christ charged him to give the sale price of his possessions to the poor.

This "spiritual pauper" was under the curse, but in his blindness he did not know it.

### 2. *The Law Cannot Justify (3:11)*

This verse contains both an apostolic observation ("it is evident") and an authoritative proof from the Old Testament ("for"). The stated principle is "that no man is justified by the law in the sight of God." Four assertions are seen. *First,* the negative indefinite pronoun (literally "no one;" *oudeis*) shows that there are no exceptions. Both Jews and Gentiles from both before and after the crucifixion of Christ are included. There is only one system of justification for both the Old Testament era and the New Testament dispensation.

*Second,* the verb literally translates as "is being justified" (*dikaioutai*). [2] It stresses what was actually going on at the time of writing.

*Third,* the prepositional phrase ("by the law")[3] designates the sphere or means by which no man could be justified. Later Paul wrote, ". . . for if there had been a law given which could have given life, verily righteousness should have been by the law" (3:21). The law was never given by God to be a means of personal salvation (Rom. 3:19–20).

*Fourth,* man may convince himself that legalism is the proper approach to God, but it has no place "in the sight of God." Since justification is the judicial act of God whereby He declares a sinner to be righteous, ultimately what He has decreed is what counts regardless of the majority opinion of unbelieving men.

To substantiate his claim Paul quoted from a key Old Testament passage: "The just shall live by faith" (cf. Hab. 2:4). This prophetic verse is quoted only three times in the New Testament (Rom. 1:17; Gal. 3:11; Heb. 10:38). Warren Wiersbe believes that the emphasis is different in the three usages, although the verse is the same.[4] The stress is on the meaning of

---

[2] It is a present passive indicative.
[3] Literally "in law" (*en nomōi*).
[4] Warren W. Wiersbe, *Be Free,* p. 70.

"just" in Romans, on the explanation of "live" in Galatians, and on the description of "faith" in Hebrews.

Since the prophet Habakkuk lived after the giving of the law but before the crucifixion of Christ, his declaration takes an added significance. In his day obedience to the law was not viewed as necessary for a justified standing before God. Again Paul argued for the continuity of the plan of redemption throughout the ages. In all dispensations justification had its source in faith, not in works. This teaching is totally compatible with Old Testament revelation.

Elsewhere Paul wrote, "But to him that worketh not, but believeth on him that justifieth the ungodly, his faith is counted for righteousness" (Rom. 4:5). To prove that principle the apostle pointed to the experiences of Abraham who lived before the law was given and of David who lived after the Mosaic legislation was instituted (Rom. 4:1–8).

### 3. *The Law Is Contrary to Faith (3:12)*

Legalism, as the method of justification and sanctification, has no place within the faith principle: "And the law is not of faith." Faith does not express itself in legalism. Faith and the law are not two sides of the same coin. Faith says that man must live before he can do, but law says that man must do before he can live. Faith charges "Believe and live," whereas the law commands "Do and live." The Judaizers claimed that the real test or evidence of true faith was in total obedience to the Mosaic regulations; however, such restrictions were not "out of faith" (*ek pisteōs*; 3:12; cf. 3:2, 5, 7, 8, 9, 11).

For Israel the sad paradox was that "they being ignorant of God's righteousness, and going about to establish their own righteousness, have not submitted themselves unto the righteousness of God" (Rom. 10:3). Their strength became their weakness. They had the law which the Gentiles did not possess. Instead of developing a greater consciousness of sin and condemnation, they became proud in their knowledge and practice of the law. It gave them a sense of superiority over the Gentiles. This unfortunate twist of circumstances created a spiritual obstacle. Paul observed:

What shall we say then? That the Gentiles, which followed not after righteousness, have attained to righteousness, even the righteousness which is of faith. But Israel, which followed after the law of righteousness, hath not attained to the law of righteousness. Wherefore? Because they sought it not by faith, but as it were by the works of the law. For they stumbled at that stumblingstone (Rom. 9:30–32).

Their dilemma became compounded. The more they tried to obey the law in order to gain justification, the farther away they went from the principle of faith.

The adversative "but" (*alla*) introduces the scriptural support for the premise that legalism has no source in the faith principle: "The man that doeth them shall live in them" (cf. Lev. 18:5). The pronoun "them" refers to "all things which are written in the book of the law" (3:10). The faith principle sets men free to become all that God meant them to be; however, legalism becomes a fence which restricts the spiritual development of men. A legalist does works within the limits prescribed by those works ("in them"). This person must spend all of his time doing and obeying. He cannot rest in what someone else has done for him. Faith says, "Done," but the law cries, "Do." The more he works, the more works there are to do. The harder he works, the more futile his effort becomes. The legalist is always under the Damocles sword of fear. He is afraid of that one moment of failure. James warned:

For whosoever shall keep the whole law, and yet offend in one point, he is guilty of all. For he that said, Do not commit adultery, said also, Do not kill. Now if thou commit no adultery, yet if thou kill, thou art become a transgressor of the law (James 2:10–11).

A definite spiritual application can be drawn from the song of the depressed coal miner, made famous by Tennessee Ernie Ford: "Sixteen tons, and what do I get: one day older and deeper in debt." When a legalist quits trying he can start trusting.

## B. Deliverance from the Law (3:13-14)

Since all men have broken the law, they are under its curse. How then can they escape this judgment? The solution is not in what they can do but in what Christ has done.

### 1. Nature of Redemption (3:13)

The Redeemer is "Christ." At His birth He was named "JESUS: for he shall save his people from their sins" (Matt. 1:21). The word for *Jesus* (*Jēsous*) is the Greek equivalent of the Hebrew *Joshua,* which means "Jehovah is salvation" or "Jehovah saves." The title *Christ* (*Christos*) means "the anointed one." God anointed Jesus with the Holy Spirit, and thus He began His ministry of preaching, teaching, and healing (Isa. 61:1-2). It climaxed in His death, resurrection, and ascension into heaven.

Four aspects of His redemptive work are enumerated. *First,* it is a finished redemption ("hath redeemed"). This verb indicates that He did it.[5] He "offered one sacrifice for sins for ever" (Heb. 10:12). It was a nonrepeatable, historical event. There are three verbs which are used to depict the biblical doctrine of redemption. The first (*agorazō*) means to pay the redemption price or to provide a ransom. It was used of purchasing slaves in the marketplace. Christ's death provided the redemption price for the sinful penalty of all men (I Cor. 6:19-20; II Peter 2:1; Rev. 5:9-10). The second (*exagarazō*), used here, means to buy out of the market. It stresses the idea of removal. The shed blood of Christ forever removed the believing sinner from the curse of the law (4:4-5). The third verb (*apolutroō*) means to release or to set free (Titus 2:14; I Peter 1:18-19).

*Second,* it is a personal redemption ("us"). Although the entire creation will enjoy the benefits of the crucifixion in the future (Rom. 8:18-23), Christ basically died for people, not for things. The personal pronoun refers to both believing Jews and Gentiles, although it pays special attention to those who found

---

[5]It is aorist active indicative.

themselves under the curse of the law through their attempts to gain justification by legalistic effort.

*Third,* it is purposeful redemption. He delivered men "from the curse of the law" (cf. 3:10). There are fringe benefits to a right relationship before God. People become mentally and emotionally stable, and fragmented families are joined together. The main intent of the cross, however, was to rescue men from spiritual condemnation and an eternity in the lake of fire.

*Fourth,* it is a substitutionary redemption. He literally became ("being made," *genomenos*) "a curse for us." The prepositional phrase shows that He did it for our benefit and that He actually suffered vicariously.[6] Christ "his own self bare our sins in his own body on the tree" (I Peter 2:24). He bare the sinner's sins, guilt, curse, and penalty. He suffered in the place of deserving sinners. Isaiah correctly prophesied:

> Surely he hath born *our* griefs, and carried *our* sorrows: yet we did esteem him stricken, smitten of God, and afflicted. But he was wounded for *our* transgressions, he was bruised for *our* iniquities: the chastisement of *our* peace was upon him; and with his stripes we are healed. . . . and the Lord hath laid on him the iniquity *of us all.* (Isa. 53:4–6).

Redemption, therefore, has been provided through His death, not by His sinless life nor by His teaching. It has been secured by only "the precious blood of Christ" (I Peter 1:19; cf. Heb. 9:22).

How could the holy Son of God become a curse? He did not become a sinner when He bore the sins of the world. Judicially He became a curse. The sinner was under the curse, and Christ took up a position between the sinner and the curse so that the curse came upon Him. The biblical support for this claim actually comes from the Mosaic law: "Cursed is every one that hangeth on a tree" (cf. Deut. 21:23). That Old Testament context demonstrated that hanging was the sign of a man who was already cursed because he had broken the law. For example, a

---

[6]The preposition is *huper,* which along with *anti* conveys personal substitution.

rebellious son was stoned to death then hung as a sign of humiliation. Both Joshua and David hung their enemies after killing them (Josh. 10:26; II Sam. 4:12). The crucifixion thus was the epitome of the humiliation of Jesus Christ.

### 2. Purposes of Redemption (3:14)

The two usages of "that" (*hina*) show the two purposes of Christ's redemptive work.[7] *First,* it gives to believers a *right position.* It was designed "that the blessing of Abraham might come on the Gentiles through Jesus Christ." The blessing of Abraham is the reality of justification by faith apart from circumcision and legalism. It was an essential part of the universal aspects of the Abrahamic covenant given to the patriarch before he was circumcised (3:8-9). The fact that Christ satisfied the righteous demands of God for sin permitted God to forgive sin and to impute a righteous standing to those who would trust only the gracious provision of Christ (Rom. 3:24-26).

*Second,* it also gives to believers a *right power* through the presence of the Holy Spirit in their lives. All Christians "receive the promise of the Spirit through faith." The justified position is not to be put into practice through legalism; rather, the Holy Spirit will produce His fruit through the trusting, yielded saint (5:22-23). The "promise of the Spirit" is a unique experience of believers in this age. Christ prayed to the Father that believers would be indwelt permanently in this dispensation (John 14:16-17). Christ promised to send the Spirit into the lives of His own after His crucifixion, resurrection, and departure into the Father's presence (John 15:26). He also assured the saints that the Father would send the Spirit in the name of Christ (John 14:26). The reception of the Holy Spirit into the life of the believing sinner occurs at the time of justification, not in some post-conversion experience (Rom. 8:9).[8] It is

[7]Technically the second purpose is a result of the fulfillment of the first purpose. Note the double usage of *hina* and no connective (*kai*).

[8]The author is aware of the transitional period in the Book of Acts when the Spirit entered the lives of certain Christians in unique ways. These unusual receptions did not provide the pattern for the normal operation of the Holy Spirit today. Consult the author's book *The Modern Tongues Movement* (Presbyterian and Reformed Publishing Co.).

that entrance which makes possible the life of sanctification "through faith." The Spirit does not come into a person's life after he has been sanctified through his own effort.

## II. THE LAW AND THE COVENANT (3:15-18)

The nation of Israel enjoyed many privileges: "to whom pertaineth the adoption, and the glory, and the covenants, and the giving of the law, and the service of God, and the promises" (Rom. 9:4). Although the law was also a covenant (*diathēkē*), it was different from the other covenants which God made with Israel (Heb. 8:9). The law was a conditional covenant. God said at Sinai: "Now therefore, if ye will obey my voice indeed, and keep my covenant, then ye shall be a peculiar treasure unto me above all people" (Exod. 19:5). In order for God to do His part the nation had to do its part; thus the Mosaic covenant was legalistic and conditional.

The major covenants, however, were unconditional: Abrahamic (Gen. 12:1-3); Palestinian (Deut. 30:1-10); Davidic (II Sam. 7:8-16); and New (Jer. 31:31-37). In these God simply promised that He would fulfill His pledge regardless of the obedience or disobedience of Israel. These unconditional covenants had their source in divine grace and were appropriated by faith, whereas the Mosaic covenant required obedience for fulfillment.

### A. Nature of a Covenant (3:15-16)

#### 1. A Human, Conditional Covenant (3:15)

The prepositional phrase ("after the manner of men")[9] refers to an accepted human principle. It points out procedures by which society governs itself. For example, men are to be paid wages for work (I Cor. 9:7-9).

Within courts of law a covenant agreed to and signed by both parties cannot be changed later by the will of only one participant. The sealed word of both men is binding upon both parties.

[9]In the Greek text it is the same prepositional phrase (*Kata anthrōpon*).

These men must respect the legal requirements of such a contract ("a man's covenant"). Quite often a person may orally agree to a contract, shake hands on it, and later back out on it. Once the contract has been ratified or "confirmed" in writing, with both signatures affixed, it becomes obligatory to both people to maintain their respective part of the bargain.

At no time in the future can one party unilaterally impose upon the covenant any new restrictions. He cannot "disannul" (*athetei*)[10] the contract. He cannot render it to be null and void. He cannot get out from under his obligations simply because he wants to. Also he cannot "add" any new restriction to the responsibilities of the other party. What was written originally must stand. If contracts could be broken easily, the worlds of business and politics would be full of chaos.

## 2. A Divine, Unconditional Covenant (3:16)

In contrast, only God must remain true to His oral and written promises contained within the unconditional covenant given to Abraham. In the ceremony of ratification only God walked through the two rows of sacrificial animals, signifying to Abraham that he only had to believe God to experience the fulfillment of the covenant blessings (Gen. 15:8–18). In this unconditional covenant God promised to do and man must only believe that God will do what He promised.

The promises were given "to Abraham and his seed." The word *seed* referred first to Isaac, the rightful heir, then to all future generations of redeemed physical descendants (Gen. 13:15–16), and ultimately to *the* seed, namely Christ. Paul argued strongly for the fact that the word was in the singular ("seed") and not in the plural ("seeds").[11] Christ is *the* son of Abraham, the rightful heir to the covenant promises (Matt. 1:1). Both the blessing of Abraham, which is justification by faith, and the promise of the Spirit come to Gentiles through Christ. Thus the law could not disannul the covenant promises

[10]Same word as "frustrate" (2:21).

[11]This verse gives strong support to the concept of verbal inspiration. The Spirit guided men even in the distinction between singular and plural.

because the latter were given to Abraham before the law and reiterated to Christ after the law.

## B. Violation of the Covenant (3:17-18)

### 1. The Law Cannot Disannul the Covenant (3:17)

If a single man cannot change a conditional covenant signed by two men, it is impossible for any man to change an unconditional covenant signed only by God.

The "covenant that was confirmed before of God in Christ" probably refers to the reaffirmation of the Abrahamic covenant to Jacob at the time the latter went down into Egypt (Gen. 46:1-4; c. 1875 B.C.). The exodus from Egypt and the giving of the law to Moses occurred 430 years later (Exod. 12:40; c. 1445 B.C.). In no way could the law "disannul" the Abrahamic covenant. To add legal conditions to an unconditional covenant would violate the principle behind the making of covenants. If legalism were added as the basis of acceptance, it would "make the promise of none effect." The promise was originally given on the basis of faith alone; thus any later addition of legalism would prove to be an injustice.

### 2. The Law Cannot Change the Inheritance (3:18)

The "inheritance" refers to the spiritual blessings contained within the universal aspects of the Abrahamic covenant (3:8). Specifically, it denotes the justified position which Abraham possessed and which would be extended eventually to all the nations of the earth. If Abraham received righteousness by faith alone, then his heirs must also receive it on the same basis.

The Judaizers claimed that obedience to "the law" was necessary to gain the inheritance. Paul argued that the addition of legalism to faith actually disannuls the concept "of promise." The law and the promise are two different means. They cannot be joined together as a dual channel for salvation.

The verb "gave" is literally "has bestowed grace" (*kecharistai*). The promise of justification by faith is not deserved by anyone. It is an unconditional gift reserved for the believing sinner. The principle of works, on the other hand, is contradictory to that of grace. When a person works he gets what he earns. In grace a person receives what he did not earn.

## QUESTIONS FOR DISCUSSION

1. In what ways can the curse of the law be illustrated from modern society?
2. Should ignorance of the law be an excuse? In society? Before God?
3. Why do men persist in their conviction that they can work their way to heaven? What approach can be used to show men the folly of this position?
4. What are some modern analogies to the ancient concept of the redemption of slaves? How can the principle of redemption be made relevant to modern society?
5. Do modern business contracts violate the principle of covenant?
6. Do Christians have a good reputation for keeping their word? Should believers always demand a written contract for purchases and services?
7. How do modern wills and inheritances illustrate the biblical concept?

# The Contrast Between Law and Faith
### Galatians 3:19–29

In review, it has been demonstrated that the law could not give the Spirit (3:1–5), could not give the righteousness of God (3:6–9), could not give the blessing (3:14), and could not change the original covenant (3:15–18). The law, however, could give a curse (3:10–13). In the remaining verses of the third chapter, Paul continued to prove the superiority of the life of faith to that of legalism.

## I. PURPOSE OF THE LAW (3:19–25)

This major section begins with a rhetorical question: "Wherefore then serveth the law?" Since the promise was given to Abraham and to Christ and since the law could not disannul the promise, why did God ever give the law to Moses and to Israel? What was its purpose? Why did not God continue to deal with the nation on the basis of the covenant of promise given to the patriarchs Abraham, Isaac, and Jacob? Why was there any change at Sinai? Such questions in the minds of his readers were doubtless anticipated by the apostle. They had to be faced and answered.

### A. The Law and the Seed (3:19–20).

#### 1. The Law Was Added (3:19a)

The verb ("it was added") literally means "it was placed before" (*prosetethē*). The Israelites were totally aware of the divine restrictions which were being imposed on them. Both before and after the law was read to them by Moses, they confessed: "All that the Lord hath said will we do" (Exod. 19:8; cf. 24:7).

Whereas divine promises are received with joy, the giving of the law produced fear (Exod. 19:16). One wrote:

> For ye are not come unto the mount that might be touched, and that burned with fire, nor unto blackness, and darkness, and tempest, and the sound of a trumpet, and the voice of words; which voice they that heard entreated that the word should not be spoken to them any more: (for they could not endure that which was commanded, and if so much as a beast touch the mountain, it shall be stoned, or thrust through with a dart: And so terrible was the sight, that Moses said, I exceedingly fear and quake) (Heb. 12:18–21).

The experience of the Christian is just the opposite. Through Christ, he has free access into the holy presence of God (Heb. 4:14–16). The believer comes out of love, not out of fear. John explained, "There is no fear in love; but perfect love casteth out fear: because fear hath torment. He that feareth is not made perfect in love" (I John 4:18).

The reason for the addition of the law was "because of transgressions."[1] It was designed to restrain fallen human nature. If no restrictions were ever placed on unregenerate wills, then sinners would manifest their position in every conceivable evil practice. The intent of the law, therefore, was to reduce the amount of sin that could be committed. In a sense, sinful man is not as *bad* as he could be (his practice), although he is as *bad off* as he can be (his position). Moral anarchy could not be tolerated by either God or man. The aim of the law was to give to sin the character of transgression and to create within the sinner a consciousness of guilt. It removed the excuse of an innate human weakness caused by evolutionary heredity or a hostile environment. It showed to man that he had willfully

[1]In the Greek text this phrase is very emphatic, occurring at the beginning of the sentence.

violated the decree of the personal, sovereign God of the universe. Elsewhere Paul observed, "For until the law sin was in the world: but sin is not imputed when there is no law" (Rom. 5:13). In a sense, sinful man could have pled ignorance as the basis of his wrongdoing. When the Ten Commandments were declared, man knew what was right and wrong from God's perspective. Human moral relatives were replaced by divine moral absolutes. Paul wrote, "Because the law worketh wrath: for where no law is, there is no transgression" (Rom. 4:15). The law was not added as a codicil to the Abrahamic covenant to serve as a further requirement to gain the promise. Rather, it prepared men for salvation. The law "entered that the offence might abound" (Rom. 5:20). When sinners realize the heinous character of their thoughts and deeds, they will know that they are incapable of doing anything to deserve eternal life.

### 2. The Law Was Temporary (3:19b)

The law served "till the seed should come to whom the promise was made." Christ is "the seed" (3:16). For Israel the law had both a beginning ("was added") and an ending. The time word *till* (*achris*) shows that the first advent of Christ terminated the historical purpose of the law. The law was designed to prepare Israel to receive the covenant promise by putting its faith in the promised seed, namely Christ.

With the death and resurrection of the Savior, the old age of the legalistic covenant ended and the new covenant of grace began (John 1:17). Concerning the cross, the apostle wrote, "Blotting out the handwriting of ordinances that was against us, which was contrary to us, and took it out of the way, nailing it to his cross" (Col. 2:14; cf. Eph. 2:15). For the individual the purpose of the law is terminated when he puts his faith in the seed of Abraham (Christ) and thus receives the promise of justification by faith alone.

### 3. The Law Needed a Mediator (3:19c)

The conditional nature of the law is revealed in the fact that "it was ordained by angels in the hand of a mediator." The "mediator" was Moses who represented both parties: man (Israel) and God. He spoke to Israel the words of God and he gave the reply of the nation back to the Lord. God and Israel did not speak directly to each other. In this sense, mediation pointed out the inferiority of the law to the promise.

In addition, "angels" took an active part at Sinai. The law was "ordained by" them (*diatageis dia*). In his sermon the deacon Stephen claimed that Israel "received the law by the disposition of angels" (Acts 7:53).[2] Although angels were not mentioned in the historical account of the giving of the law, Moses at the end of his life commented, "The Lord came from Sinai . . . and he came with ten thousands of saints: from his right hand went a fiery law for them" (Deut. 33:2; cf. Ps. 68:17).[3] Angels definitely represented the divine interest in the proceedings. It is conceivable that the giving of the Mosaic law was the basis for this scriptural observation: "For if the word spoken by angels was stedfast, and every transgression and disobedience received a just recompense of reward" (Heb. 2:2). In any case, the law needed a mediator to bring the two parties together.

### 4. The Promise Needed No Mediator (3:20)

A mediator represents two parties, not just one ("Now a mediator is not a mediator of one"). This procedure is absolutely essential in the ratification of a conditional covenant between two differing interests.

An unconditional covenant, however, needs no mediator. It depends solely upon God ("but God is one"). The giving of a gift depends only upon the desire of the giver. The intended recipient may accept or reject the gift but he cannot propose any restrictions upon the giver. So it is with the gift of imputed righteousness. Totally undeserved, it may be accepted or rejected by the sinner, but he cannot add to the requirements for the giving of eternal life.

Christ is the mediator between God and man (I Tim. 2:5). He is the mediator of a new and better covenant (Heb. 8:6; 9:15,

---

[2]The Greek word for "disposition" (*diatagas*) is based upon the same stem as that for "ordained."

[3]The Septuagint, the Greek version of the Hebrew Old Testament, adds these words to this verse: ". . . at his right hand were angels with him."

12:24). His role as mediator, however, is different. He is both divine and human. He brings together God and man in His person and in His redemptive death. As divine He represents God to man; and as human He represents man to God. Thus the conditions for justification by faith are centered in Him. For man He is the only way to the Father (John 14:6). For God He was the means of reconciling the world unto the Father (II Cor. 5:19).

## B. The Law and the Promises (3:21-22)

### 1. The Law Is Not Against the Promises (3:21a)

Again Paul raised a rhetorical question: "Is the law then against the promises of God?" Since justification by legalistic works is the main obstacle to the reception of justification by faith, it would appear that "the law" was actually an opponent to "the promises." The righteousness of the law, produced by self, is often the main deterrent to the righteousness of God, imputed through faith in Christ (Phil. 3:9). This deplorable situation, however, is not the fault of the law; rather it is caused by man's misunderstanding and misuse of the divine intent behind the law.

Since God gave both the promise to Abraham and the law to Moses, the two covenants must complement each other. God is never His own enemy. He never contradicts Himself. This is the reason why the apostle immediately reacted: "God forbid."[4] The law was not given to replace or to replenish the promise; rather it was supposed to prepare men to receive the promise.

### 2. The Law Cannot Give Life (3:21b)

For the sake of argument, the apostle then proposed a hypothesis which is actually contrary to fact: "... for if there had been a law given which could have given life, verily righteousness should have been by the law."[5] Theoretically salva-

---

[4]Literally "May it not come to pass" (*mē genoito*).

[5]This contrary to fact conditional sentence is indicated by the usage of *ei* ("if") in the protasis and the presence of the particle *an* in the apodosis. Both parts employ secondary tenses: the aorist *edothē* and the imperfect *ēn*.

Ruins of an aqueduct near Antioch of Pisidia.

tion could have come through obedience to a law if men would have had the ability and the willingness to keep it. Therein lies the problem. The law could tell men what to do but it could not supply the power to do it. The moral impotence of men dominated by sin made legalism an impossible foundation or channel for salvation. Men, who were dead in trespasses and sins, needed to be quickened by God because they could not spiritually resurrect themselves (Eph. 2:1–5). Elsewhere Paul wrote, "For what the law could not do, in that it was weak through the flesh, God sending his own Son in the likeness of sinful flesh, and for sin, condemned sin in the flesh: that the righteousness of the law might be fulfilled in us" (Rom. 8:3–4).

The law did contain promises for the enjoyment of life on earth. God said, "All the commandments which I command thee this day shall ye observe to do, that ye may live, and multiply, and go in and possess the land which the Lord sware unto your fathers" (Deut. 8:1). To experience the material blessings of God within the Promised Land, Israel had to obey the law. Their subsequent rebellion brought defeat and dispersion; however their unconditional covenant relationship was sustained by the faithfulness of God in the midst of their sin.

### 3. *The Law Prepares Men to Receive the Promise (3:22)*

The law is "scripture." As such, it is God-breathed and "profitable for doctrine, for reproof, for correction, for instruction in righteousness" (II Tim. 3:16). In its divine purpose, it has "concluded all under sin." The verb "hath concluded" (*sunekleisen*) means to shut up together on all sides. It was used of the miraculous catch of fish that was "inclosed" [same word] within the net. All men, thus, are numbered together. There are no exceptions. They are "all" equally trapped within the dominion of sin.

The law was given to create within man a consciousness that he was completely enveloped in sin with no ability to rescue himself from his spiritual dilemma. The Scripture proves that both Jews and Gentiles are all "under sin" (cf. Rom. 3:9). In such a condition, men must stop making excuses for their sin and start admitting their guilt to God (Rom. 3:19). Unregenerate man is imprisoned as a slave to his cruel taskmaster of sin. He stands in real need of pardon and redemption. Elsewhere Paul observed, "For God hath concluded them all in unbelief, that he might have mercy upon all" (Rom. 11:32).

The purpose for the conclusion is seen in the word *that* (*hina*): "that the promise by faith of Jesus Christ might be given to them that believe." When sinners stop trying to save themselves and start trusting in Christ to save them, the law has fulfilled its purpose in their lives. What the law was unable to give because of the impotence of man (3:21), God is able to give because of the power of the crucified, resurrected Christ. The promise is given "to them that believe," not to them that work (Rom. 4:5).

## C. The Law and Faith (3:23–25)

### 1. The Law Was a Guard (3:23)

All unregenerate men are under the curse (3:10), under sin (3:22), and "under the law" (3:23). Although these relationships have some distinctiveness, Kent remarked that "these are not totally different, for the law contained the standards which had been transgressed and thus was the proof that sin had been committed."[6] All unsaved men are under sin regardless of whether they have had personal contact with the Mosaic law. The isolated heathen has rejected the revelation of God in nature and thereby demonstrated his slavery to sin (Rom. 1:18–32).

As a legalistic Jew, Paul then inserted himself into the argument (note the usage of "we" and "our"). In their unsaved lives, both the Galatians and the apostle "were kept under the law." They were literally under constant surveillance.[7] They were in the prison house of sin with no way of escape. The law was like a jailor or a sentry, watching every act of moral disobedience. They were being guarded at all times.

[6]Homer A. Kent Jr., *The Freedom of God's Sons,* p. 104.
[7]The verb is in the imperfect tense. Literally "we were being kept."

This state of protective custody occurred "before faith came." The definite article *the* appears before the noun, thus literally "before the faith came." *Historically* this phrase refers to the coming of the seed, Jesus Christ, and His subsequent redemptive death and resurrection. The basic doctrines of fundamental Christianity are entitled "the faith" (I Tim. 4:1; Jude v. 3). The penal function of the law ended with the introduction of the new age of grace and faith. *Personally* the phrase ("the faith") points back to that faith exercised by the believing sinner (3:22). It is the subjective appropriation of the objective fact that Christ came to deliver from the curse of the law and to impart His promise of righteousness by faith.

In their sinful position, they are also "shut up unto the faith which should afterward be revealed." The participle *shut up* (*sugkekleismenoi*) is the same word earlier translated as "concluded" (3:22). This legal confinement was not intended to give the moral prisoners a sense of fulfillment or satisfaction; rather it promoted an expectation of release from one other than himself.

## 2. The Law Was a Schoolmaster (3:24–25)

In ancient cultures a "schoolmaster" was usually a slave who was responsible for the education and protection of a child who had not yet reached adulthood. Literally the word means a "child guide" or a "child leader or conductor" (*paidagōgos*). In some cases, the guardian of the child was not actually the teacher. Quite often the *paidagōgos* was a teacher's aide who took the child from the home to the school. He also watched over the behavior of the child at home.

Through analogy the law became[8] a "schoolmaster." For Paul and others (note "our") the law taught them about themselves: about the wrongness of their behavior, about their relationship to others, and about their position before God.

The law performed two tasks. *First,* it brought men "unto Christ." The law, when properly used, does not lead a person to itself nor does it inform a person that he is perfect. Rather, it

---

[8]The verb "was" is *gegonen,* meaning "it has come to be."

conducts men to the person and redemptive work of Christ. *Second,* the purpose for guiding men to Christ is "that [they] might be justified by faith." The law could not provide such justification because it does not operate out of the faith principle (3:12). The law, recognizing its moral limitations, nevertheless serves as the divine-human instrument to create the need for justification.

When a person comes to faith in Christ, he is "no longer under a schoolmaster." The dispensational responsibility of the law ended at the cross and its personal role as custodian terminates when a believing sinner becomes a spiritual son of God. In Christ the believer is "not under the law, but under grace." As natural death frees a wife from the law of her husband, so spiritual identification with Christ in His crucifixion and resurrection has set a justified sinner free from his positions under law and under sin.

Thus, the law as a *paidagōgos* performed a needed function before justification, but it has no authority over the regenerated child of God. The redeemed sinner does not have to obey the law to maintain his justified position or to achieve sanctification. Of course, at all times he is "not without law to God, but under the law to Christ" (I Cor. 9:21). He must never be morally lawless; rather he should always be submissive to the righteous, eternal law of God which transcends all ages and which reflects the holy character of God.

## II. POSITION UNDER FAITH (3:26-29)

When a person was under the works of the law he soon found himself to be under the curse and under sin. Now Paul wanted to show the favorable position of the sinner who has been justified by faith in Christ.

### A. Sons of God (3:36)

The first privilege is that of being the sons of God. The verse actually reads "sons" (*huoi*) rather than "children" (*tekna*). Although these two terms are used interchangeably by many, they do have distinctive meanings of their own. A believing sinner becomes a child of God through regeneration or the new birth (John 1:12), whereas a regenerated sinner becomes a son of God by the act of spiritual adoption (cf. 4:5). A "child" is a child because he has the nature of his parent within him, but he is still immature and must grow into adulthood. In real life a "child" does not have the mature responsibilities and privileges of sonship until he reaches a predetermined age (sixteen, eighteen, or twenty-one). When a businessman brings his son into full partnership (e.g. John Doe and Son), the male who has been a child all along becomes a son in the legal sense of the word.

In spiritual experience a person becomes a child and a son at the same instant. A regenerated child is immediately put into the position of sonship whereby he enjoys all of the privileges and responsibilities of sonship. The noun "adoption" means "to put into the position of sons" (*huiothesian*). This act was determined by God in eternity past (Eph. 1:5) and finalized by the operation of the Holy Spirit at the point of conversion (4:6; Rom. 8:15). Christ really came "to redeem them that were under the law, that we might receive the adoption of sons" (4:5). As long as a person was under the schoolmaster of law he could never be regarded as a son.

The means of becoming a son is "by faith in Christ Jesus." This statement refers to the event of initial faith which secures redemption. The full benefits of sonship, however, will not be enjoyed until the believer has received his new immortal, incorruptible body. Paul observed, ". . . but ourselves also, which have the first fruits of the Spirit, even we ourselves groan within ourselves, waiting for the adoption, to wit, the redemption of our body" (Rom. 8:23). Sonship thus is possible only because one has his position in Christ, and because the Holy Spirit is in him. This truth is a blessing of the Abrahamic covenant promises rather than of the law (cf. 3:14).

## B. Baptized into Christ (3:27a)

All genuine believers "have been baptized into Christ." Through the ministry of the Holy Spirit they have been spiritually placed or immersed into Christ with the result that their new position is in Christ. Paul wrote elsewhere, "Therefore if any man be in Christ, he is a new creature: old things are passed away, behold, all things are become new" (II Cor. 5:17). Once the sinner was condemned, but now he has become "accepted in the beloved" (Eph. 1:6). Throughout the Pauline Epistles the believer's standing before God is designated as being "in Christ." If they are *in* Christ, how did they get *into* Christ? The act of spiritual baptism secured this result.

What kind of baptism is described in this verse? Although some identify it as water baptism,[9] it doubtless refers to the baptism in the Holy Spirit. All believers possess "one Lord, one faith, one baptism" (Eph. 4:5). It is not true that all believers have experienced water baptism or that those who have been baptized in water have all been baptized in the same way.[10] To get into the "one body" (Eph. 4:4), the true church, a person must be baptized in the Holy Spirit. This act is not a post-conversion experience but rather a work of God which occurs at the moment of conversion. There are not two groups of believers today: those who are saved but who are not in the one body and others who are both saved and in the body. All believers are in the one body, the true church (Matt. 16:18; Eph. 1:22–23). Paul clearly commented:

> For as the body is one, and hath many members, and all the members of that one body, being many, are one body: so also is Christ. For by [in] one Spirit are we all baptized into one body, whether we be Jews or Gentiles, whether we bond or free; and have been all made to drink into one Spirit (I Cor. 12:12–13).

The baptism in the Holy Spirit thus achieves two goals. *First,* it unites all regenerated sinners within the one body of the true church. *Second,* it places the believer into a spiritual position within Christ where he finds acceptance before God. He is now

[9] A. T. Robertson, *Word Pictures in the New Testament,* IV, 298.

[10] For example: sprinkling, pouring, immersed once backwards, or immersed three times forward.

both in Christ and in the body of Christ. All are "members of [Christ's] body, of his flesh, and of his bones" (Eph. 5:30).

## C. Put on Christ (3:27b)

Grammatically the verse reads: "You, as many as were baptized into Christ, have put on Christ." As clothing, Christ is put around the believer, whereas in spiritual baptism, the believer is placed into the Savior. At conversion the sinner puts off the filthy rags of self-righteousness and puts on the righteousness of God, even Christ Himself (Isa. 64:6; I Cor. 1:30). He must then manifest his new position by a new practice of life. He must put off the old man with its sinful habits and put on the new man of godly behavior (Rom. 13:14; Eph. 4:22–24; Col. 3:9–10).

This change of spiritual clothing was taken from a cultural custom.[11] In ancient times a Roman lad wore the *toga praetexta,* a toga with an elaborately embroidered purple hem. When the boy reached manhood he put off this sign of immaturity and put on the white toga. Thus, under law, a person could never merit the clothing of spiritual sonship.

## D. Oneness in Christ (3:28)

All believers are "one in Christ Jesus." This is positional oneness and equality. In Him there is no spiritual superiority or inferiority. All mundane divisions are eliminated: racial ("Jew nor Greek"), social ("bond nor free"), and sexual ("male nor female"). The man is not more accepted in Christ than the woman nor is the Jew more justified than the Gentile. All share the same standing before God.

The removal of classifications refers only to the spiritual position, however. People do not lose their distinctiveness within the functional order of society. A woman is a woman both before and after conversion, and so is a man a man. Within the oneness of the divine essence, there is an equality of

[11]Cited by Kent, *op. cit.,* p. 107.

the persons of the Godhead, but there nevertheless remains an order for the execution of the divine purpose of redemption. The Father is the head of Christ and the former sent the latter into the world. In the same sense, the man and the woman are one in Christ, but the headship of the man over the woman remains in order to carry out the divine purpose for the home and for the local church (I Cor. 11:3).

### E. Abraham's Seed (3:29)

The logic of this concluding verse is convincing. *First,* all believers belong to Christ ("and if ye be Christ's"). They have been baptized into Him, clothed with Him, and are in Him. *Second,* since Christ is the seed of Abraham (3:16), then all who are in Christ are also "Abraham's seed." Christ was seminally present in the patriarch when the covenant promises were given to Abraham; thus the believer was spiritually present in the Savior at that time. *Third,* all believers along with Christ are "heirs according to the promise." What was promised to Abraham was also promised to future generations who would be justified by faith in the same way. Since legalism was not part of the Abrahamic covenant obligation, then the charge of the Judaizers has been demonstrated to be false.

## QUESTIONS FOR DISCUSSION

1. Are modern laws added because of transgressions? Do present laws encourage or lessen crime? How can they be changed?
2. Should a Christian ever break a legal binding contract? Should agreements ever be made without a witness?
3. What systems of religion teach that they have laws which can be kept to gain salvation?
4. Why do many believe that they can keep the Ten Commandments or the Sermon on the Mount? In this relationship discuss the approach that Christ used in dealing with the rich young ruler.

5. What contemporary analogies to the schoolmaster can be used?
6. Do parents try to run the lives of their children after the latter have become adults? Is this good or bad? Why?
7. How do the movements for racial, social, and sexual equality affect fundamental Christianity? Is there discrimination in local churches today?

# 8

# The Contrast Between Sonship and Servanthood
## *Galatians 4:1–11*

In cultures which practiced slavery, there were obvious differences between a servant and a master, between a son of a slave and a son of a slave owner. Although the servant may have possessed greater physical strength and innate intelligence than an owner's son, the servant was still regarded as an inferior person. The servant was under orders to obey, and the son was free to enjoy the provision of the father.

In his argument for the superiority of Christ, the author of Hebrews pointed out that "Moses verily was faithful in all his house as a servant" but that the Savior was "a son over his own house" (Heb. 3:5-6). A slave is never free to do anything voluntarily; rather he is always obligated to obey laws.

Although regeneration changed the spiritual position of a slave, it did not eliminate his social status. He was still a slave in the sight of men. Many of the Epistles contained valuable counsel for the converted servants and slave owners (Eph. 6:5-9; Col. 3:22—4:1). Paul encouraged Philemon to receive the recently saved Onesimus "not now as servant, but above a servant, as a brother beloved" (Philem. v. 16).

The cultural background of the first century thus provided a perfect analogy between the principles of spiritual sonship and those of spiritual bondage.

## I. BIBLICAL SONSHIP (4:1-7)

A genuine believer is both a child of Abraham and a son of God (3:7, 26). These concepts, introduced earlier in the book, will now be developed in greater detail.

## A. Preparation for Sonship (4:1-3)

There is a difference between a child and a son. It takes much time for a totally dependent infant to develop into an independent son. This period of preparation is now used as an illustration of the person who has been under the law.

### 1. A Child Is Like a Servant (4:1)

The opening personal reference ("Now I say") serves to join the previous section with this topic. The apostle had used this literary device earlier in his discussion about the nature of a covenant (3:17).

All believers are spiritual "heirs" (3:29). They inherit the promises of the Abrahamic covenant, including justification by faith (3:14, 16, 18).

In natural life a potential heir does not receive an inheritance until a rich relative dies or until he reaches a stipulated age. For example, the prodigal son enjoyed his inheritance even before his father had died (Luke 15:12). No rational father, however, would give millions of dollars to an infant or an adolescent. Oftentimes he puts large sums of money into a trust fund which the child cannot control until he reaches a responsible age.

In spiritual life both the provision and the appropriation of an inheritance have been made possible through the death of Jesus Christ. The Book of Hebrews states:

> For where a testament is, there must also of necessity be the death of the testator. For a testament is of force after men are dead: otherwise it is of no strength at all while the testator liveth (Heb. 9:16–17).

Unlike natural life, though, a person is able to receive his inheritance at the very moment of spiritual birth. He enjoys the privileges of sonship immediately.

In this section, the reception of an inheritance is set for a prearranged time (cf. 4:2). Before that event occurs the recipient is designated in three ways. *First,* he is "the heir." The usage of the definite article shows that he is the only child within the family. *Second,* he is a "child" (*nēpios*). This word is used usually for an infant, a minor who does not even talk. *Third,* he is "lord of all." Since he has the nature of his father within him, he possesses the birthright. He is the potential lord of his father's estate although he must wait before he will be able to exercise his lordship in a practical way.

The heir, however, has two problems. *First,* he cannot receive his inheritance "as long as he is a child." He must wait for the time when he will be formally viewed as mature, as a responsible son. *Second,* in his childish condition, he "differeth nothing from a servant." A servant has no inheritance, and neither does the childish heir. A servant is in a state of subservience and obedience, and so is the childish heir. The latter must obey both the regulations of the house and the directives of his "tutors and governors" (4:2). Thus while he is under legal servitude he cannot receive his inheritance. Paul effectively used this analogy to show that as long as a person put himself under obligation to the Mosaic law, he could never receive a spiritual inheritance. The main thrust of the Judaizers, consequently, was discredited.

## 2. A Child Is Under Supervision (4:2)

The life of the heir is divided into two different periods of time: the years of supervision and the era of sonship. The pivotal event which separates them is "the time appointed of the father." Two observations are made concerning these early years.

*First,* the identity of the supervisors is given. He is "under tutors and governors." The "tutors" (*epitropous*) are guardians of minors or orphans. They have been entrusted by their lords with the payment of monies. For example, the "Lord of the vineyard saith unto his steward [same word], Call the laborers, and give them their hire" (Matt. 20:8). The Greek word for "governors" (*oikonomous*)[1] literally means "house laws." The word, normally translated as "steward," refers to a manager of an estate or property (Luke 12:42). Erastus was actually the "chamberlain" or steward (same word) of the city of Corinth (Rom. 16:23). Paul saw himself as a steward "of the mysteries of God" (I Cor. 4:1–2). In this context, the heir is *under* these supervisors who had been directly appointed by his father. He had to obey them and the laws for the management of the household in the same way as the regular servants.

*Second,* the *time* of supervision was restricted "until the time appointed of the father." Each family was different, thus the designated time varied. According to Roman law, however, a tutor had charge of a child until the latter became fourteen years of age; then a curator guided the young man until he was twenty-five. The time was set by "the father" both in oral instruction and in a written will. The time of legal sonship, then, was not affected by the premature death of the father.

### 3. A Child Is in Bondage (4:3)

The opening words ("even so we") point out a spiritual analogy to the cultural custom of the position of heirs under supervision. Three facts are stated about the bondage. *First,* the *objects* of bondage included Paul. Before sonship an heir was *under* the law of the stewards; before justification by faith Paul and the Jewish believers were *under* the bondage of the Mosaic law. The usage of the personal pronoun ("we") primarily refers to the Jewish group at Galatia (cf. 3:23–25). The apostle seems to use "ye" when both Jewish and Gentile Christians are grouped together (3:26–29; 4:8).

*Second,* the temporal clause ("when we were children" [*nēpioi*]) points to the *time* of bondage when Paul and the Jewish residents of Galatia were unconverted. Of course the Jews did not equate themselves with moral children as they aggressively tried to obey the law. In his former life as a Pharisee the apostle doubtless made the same confession as the

[1]The word *dispensation* is also based upon this word (Eph. 1:10).

religious opponents of Christ: "We be Abraham's seed, and were never in bondage to any man" (John 8:33). Now from the advantage of spiritual hindsight Paul recognized that he could have never received the blessings of heirship while he was in subjection to the righteousness of the law.

*Third,* the *scope* of bondage was "under the elements of the world." The verbal construction ("were in bondage") shows a permanent spiritual condition.[2] The preposition ("under") continues the analogy: under tutors and governors (4:2), under the elements of the world (4:3), and under the law (4:5).

What are these elements? They include the basic, fundamental principles of legalistic Judaism. They are later called the "weak and beggarly elements" (4:9). Elsewhere Paul warned against the threat of being spoiled by "the rudiments [same word] of the world" (Col. 2:8). Through regeneration, a justified believer is actually dead to them (Col. 2:20). He is under no obligation to obey them. These "elements" (*stoicheia*) were the same regulations that the Judaizers were attempting to impose upon the Galatian converts. The philosophy "of the world" stresses the ability of man to do something to gain acceptance with his God. For generations unconverted men have emphasized the importance of keeping the Ten Commandments, the Sermon on the Mount, or the Golden Rule as the means of obtaining personal salvation.

Packer, however, believed that "the elements of the world" was "an astrological name for the angels who ruled the stars, here applied to Satan's hosts."[3] In some ways, it could correspond to the signs of the zodiac (cf. 4:10). It is true that Satan controls the minds of men through religious and pseudoscientific legalism, but the problem at Galatia centered around the Mosaic law as the means of justification before the true God. The Jewish calendar of ritualistic observances must not be equated with the concepts of astrology.

---

[2]It is a periphrastic form (*hēmen dedoulōmenoi*), the usage of the perfect passive participle with the imperfect of *eimi.* The words for *servant* and *bondage* come from the same Greek root.

[3]James I. Packer, "Galatians," *The Biblical Expositor,* p. 299.

## B. Means of Sonship (4:4-5)

The redemptive purpose of God is the source of the deliverance of man from his bondage to the law. The eternal decree was effectively executed by the Son through His entrance into the world and His subsequent vicarious crucifixion.

### 1. The Incarnation of the Son (4:4)

Five features of this great event are enumerated. *First,* the time of the incarnation is indicated in the opening temporal clause ("when the fullness of the time was come"). This historical event corresponds to the cultural "time appointed of the father" (4:2). Just as the human father selected a date at which the child would become a son, so the divine Father chose a time when the world would pass from its childhood under legal supervision to a period of spiritual sonship. The events of Christ's incarnation, death, and resurrection marked the change from the dispensation of law to the age of grace. Daniel predicted that the age of the Messiah could actually be discerned by the computation of years from the Persian decree to rebuild Jerusalem (Dan. 9:25). The Messiah was to come during the domination of the fourth Gentile world power over Israel: Babylon, Persia, Greece, and Rome (Dan. 2:31-45; 7:1-14). The Magi recognized the significance of their era (Matt. 2:1-2), but the religious leaders were ignorant of the signs of the times (Matt. 16:1-5; Luke 19:41-44).

*Second,* the incarnation was a commissioned event. The verb "sent forth" (*exapesteilen*) literally means "to send away from with a commission." The addition of the prefix (*ex*) shows that God sent His son *out* of heaven to earth with a commission to turn servants into sons. Christ was God's apostle to a world of sinners.[4] The departure from heaven to earth shows that Christ actually existed before Mary conceived in her womb.

*Third,* the person sent was the Son of God ("his Son"). He did not become the Son of God at His human birth, baptism,

---

[4]The word *apostle* is based on the verb *sent forth.*

crucifixion, or resurrection; rather He was, is, and always shall be the eternal Son of God. Agur asked concerning the creator God, "What is his name, and what is his son's name?" (Prov. 30:4). The sending and the giving of the Son are synonymous (John 3:16). Within the trinitarian oneness of God there is an equality of Persons; however, there is a voluntary subordination of function to carry out the divine counsel. God the Father sent the Son. This occurred once and only once in the history of the world.[5] No other person could have ever be sent.

*Fourth,* the means of the incarnation was through the virgin birth ("made of a woman"). Several evangelicals argue that this statement only demonstrates that Christ had a complete and perfect humanity.[6] Paul, however, later used a different verb to depict natural birth (*gennaō;* 4:23). The verb "made" (*genomenon*) is used elsewhere of Christ's incarnation: "And the Word was made flesh" (John 1:14). He was the promised seed of the woman who would destroy Satan (Gen. 3:15). His virgin conception and birth out of Mary fulfilled the Jewish expectation: "Behold, a virgin shall conceive, and bear a son, and shall call his name Immanuel" (Isa. 7:14; cf. Matt. 1:23).[7] The eternal Son of God came to be human out of Mary. This birth was necessary to establish Himself as the legitimate Son of David, the son of Abraham (Matt. 1:1). By the overshadowing ministry of the Holy Spirit, He took on Himself a human nature without receiving a sinful tendency (Luke 1:26–38).

*Fifth,* His incarnation occurred "under the law." He came to where men were. Born of a Jewish woman, He said that He came to fulfill the law, not to destroy it (Matt. 5:17). He was circumcised at the age of eight days (Luke 2:21), presented in the temple at the age of forty days (Luke 2:22), and took a pilgrimage to Jerusalem at Passover when He was twelve (Luke 2:41–52). In His adult experience He never violated the

[5]Indicated by the aorist tense.

[6]Everett F. Harrison, *The Wycliffe Bible Commentary,* p. 1293; Homer A. Kent, *The Freedom of God's Sons,* p. 111; and A. T. Robertson, *Word Pictures in the New Testament,* IV, 301.

[7]For a detailed discussion of the incarnation, consult the author's book, *The Virgin Birth: Doctrine of Deity* (Thomas Nelson Publishers).

law although He did break the pharisaical interpretation of what the law demanded.

## 2. The Redemption of the Son (4:5)

Two purposes of Christ's incarnation and crucifixion are set forth here.[8] They both manifest the end result of the sending of the Son by the Father. *First,* Christ died "to redeem them that were under the law." Men are both bought out of the curse of the law and out of their position under law (3:13). They have been completely set free from any further obligations to legalism. If Jews were removed from their condition under the law, then why did the pagan Gentile converts want to be placed under it?

*Second,* His redemptive death made it possible "that we might receive the adoption of sons." To be put into a position of legal sonship, one must be taken out of a status of legal supervision. The analogy from culture proved that axiom (4:1–2). No man could receive sonship while he was still under the law, thus no man could ever be justified by both faith and works. Christ thus came to taste death for every man, to bring many sons into glory, and to "deliver them who through fear of death were all their lifetime subject to bondage" (Heb. 2:9, 10, 15). Sonship comes after redemption from legalism.

## C. Confirmation of Sonship (4:6–7)

How can a person know that he is a son? What are the evidences of the fact that he is no longer a spiritual child under legal supervision? The opening causal clause ("because ye are sons") introduces the reader to two spiritual realities that will exist in the life of every genuine Christian. They are results of sonship which actually confirm that position.

## 1. Awareness of the Father (4:6)

The living reality of the Father-son relationship is achieved through a series of three steps. *First,* "God hath sent forth the

[8]Indicated by the double usage of the purpose conjunction *hina* ("to" and "that"). Actually, the second purpose is a result of the first one.

Spirit of his Son." The Spirit is both the Spirit of the Father and of the Son (Phil. 1:19). He has been sent into the world by both the Father and the Son (John 14:26; 15:26). He has come to glorify the Son (John 16:14). God the Father sent the Son to provide the position of sons (4:4) and He sent the Spirit to activate the practice of sonship.[9]

*Second,* the Spirit is present within the "hearts" of believers. This word does not refer to the physical organ, but rather to the seat of personality. It is the inner man (Eph. 3:16). In fact, the entire body of the Christian is indwelt by the Holy Spirit (I Cor. 6:19–20). It is impossible to be a son of God without having the sign of sonship within. Paul wrote elsewhere: "Now if any man have not the Spirit of Christ, he is none of his" (Rom. 8:9). Thus the presence of the Spirit within the heart of a believer must occur at the moment of sonship, not in a postconversion experience. There are no sons without the Spirit.

*Third,* the Spirit Himself cries out to the Father from within the believer. The participle ("crying") refers to the Spirit, and not to the Christian, in this verse. However the believer also cries out: "For ye have not received the spirit of bondage again to fear: but ye have received the Spirit of adoption, whereby we cry, Abba, Father" (Rom. 8:15). Thus the Spirit through the believer causes the new son of God to exclaim the spiritual fatherhood of God. The word *Abba*[10] is Aramaic, whereas the word *Father* is based upon the Greek *patēr*.

## 2. Heirship with the Son (4:7)

This verse indicates a sequence from "servant" to "son" to "heir." In the cultural analogy the sequence went from heir to servant to son (4:1). The main difference between the two is that all men were born as spiritual paupers, enslaved to the bondage of sin. They were slaves at the outset. God had to redeem them, to regenerate them as children, and to adopt them at the same moment. In the natural life sonship takes

---

[9]The verbs "sent forth" are identical.

[10]It is neuter in gender (*krazon*), agreeing with the neuter Greek word for Spirit (*pneuma*).

years to accomplish, but in the spiritual life it occurs in an instant.

Wiersbe cites these contrasts between a son and a servant.[11] The son has the same nature as the Father, but the servant does not (II Peter 1:4). The son has a father, but a servant has a master. The son obeys out of love, but the servant out of fear (Rom. 5:5; Gal. 5:22). The son has a future, but the servant has none. The son is rich, but the servant is poor. The son enjoys the riches of: grace (Eph. 1:7), goodness (Rom. 2:4), and wisdom (Rom. 11:33). In fact, he possesses all riches in Christ (Phil. 4:19).

Sonship carries within that relationship heirship. Every believer is "an heir of God through Christ." All that belongs to the Father belongs to the Son, and all that belongs to the Son belongs to the Christian. Since Christ had to suffer to gain His glorification, then all believers should expect to go through the same means to gain their inheritance (Rom. 8:17).

## II. PAGAN SERVANTHOOD (4:8-11)

Paul wanted to prove that legalism was no better than paganism. In principle they were identical because both required strict observance of rituals and laws to gain salvation. To the apostle the Judaizers were similar to the pagan religious priests who once supervised the Galatians before their conversion.

### A. Their Pagan Past (4:8)

The Galatians were now sons, but once they were slaves within the system of pagan legalism. The opening words ("Howbeit then") are used to remind the converts from paganism of their former lives.

#### 1. They Did Not Know the True God (4:8a)

They "knew not God." They did not know intellectually or experientially the trinitarian God of the Scriptures. They did

[11]Warren W. Wiersbe, *Be Free*, pp. 92-93.

not know who He was nor what He demanded. They were "without God in the world" (Eph. 2:12). They walked ". . . in the vanity of their mind, having the understanding darkened, being alienated from the life of God through the ignorance that is in them, because of the blindness of their heart" (Eph. 4:17–18).

### 2. They Served False Gods (4:8b)

The verb ("ye did service," *edouleusate*) means "to serve as a slave."[12] Their bondage to false gods was expressed through their pagan religious system of temples, priests, sacrifices, feasts, and legal restrictions.

They worshiped such gods as Jupiter and Mercury (Acts 14:11–13), but these gods did not actually exist. They "by nature are no gods." Even though pagans may give personal names to the gods of their polytheistic system and to the idols which represent those gods, this does not mean that their gods actually do live (I Cor. 8:5–6). In fact, they are worshiping Satan and the demons through these faulty misrepresentations (I Cor. 10:20). There is only one true God regardless of what men may think or believe.

## B. Their Present Position (4:9a)

The opening words ("But now") show the contrast between their present religious experience ("now") with their past unbelief ("then").

### 1. They Know the True God

Once they knew not God, but now they know Him. There is an obvious distinction between the negative and the positive. Also the two verbs for "knowing" are different. As pagans they knew not (*eidotes*) God, but now they "have known" Him (*gnontes*). The second verb stresses an experiential, personal knowledge. To know God in this way is to have eternal life. Jesus said, "And this is life eternal, that they might know thee,

---

[12]The words for *slave* and *service* come from the same Greek root.

the only true God, and Jesus Christ, whom thou has sent" (John 17:3). When the apostle was at Lystra he exhorted the pagans to "turn from these vanities unto the living God" (Acts 14:15). When they repented and believed, they knew God in salvation.

### 2. *The True God Knows Them*

A believer both knows God and is known by Him ("or rather are known of God").[13] The former views salvation from man's perspective, whereas the second sees it from God's sovereign purpose. Christ said that He knew His sheep by name (John 10:3, 27). Paul claimed that "the Lord knoweth them that are his" (II Tim. 2:19). Saving knowledge has two sides: human accountability through response and divine sovereignty through choice. We know Him because He first knew us (Rom. 8:29; cf. I John 4:19).

## C. Their Perilous Problem (4:9b–10)

### 1. *They Were Turning to Legalism (4:9b)*

The Galatians were ignorant of the significance of their actions. To shake them out of their mental and spiritual lethargy Paul fired a challenging question at them: "How turn ye again to the weak and beggarly elements . . . ?" The verb, which is in the present tense (*epistrephete*), shows that they were moving into legalistic practices (4:10) but that they had not yet submitted to circumcision (5:2). The adverb ("again") reveals the equation of the principles of pagan legalism with those of Judaizing legalism. They were turning back to a system of works from which they had been saved.

They were turning from a position of strength to that of weakness. The "elements" (*stoicheia*) refer to laws and regulations (cf. 4:3). They are "weak" in that they are powerless to provide redemption. They are "beggarly" in that they cannot supply a spiritual inheritance.

---

[13]The two verbs in verse 9 are both from *ginōskō*, whereas the verb in verse 8 is from *oida*.

### 2. *They Were Desiring to be Slaves (4:9c)*

Their problem rested within their wills ("ye desire;" *thelete*). In the past their wills were dominated by demons; now in the present, their volition was being deceived by the Judaizers. The usage of the adverb ("again") further manifests the identification of the two systems of legalism. The verbal concepts of enslavement ("to be in bondage" and "did service") are also the same.[14]

### 3. *They Were Observing Ritualistic Feasts (4:10)*

The verb ("ye observe") shows that they were presently involved in the observance of the Mosaic calendar. The "days" include the weekly sabbaths and the daily fasts. The "months" refer to the celebration of the beginning of new months (Num. 10:10). The "times" or seasons (*kairous*) embrace the major feasts, such as Passover, Pentecost, and Tabernacles. The "years" are the sabbatical year, which occurred every seventh year, and the year of jubilee, which happened every fifty years.

These rituals, appropriate in a former age for Israel, anticipated their fulfillment in the redemptive work of Christ (Col. 2:16–17). Paul strongly warned against any return to such rites for a person who had been justified by faith.

## D. Paul's Perplexity (4:11)

Paul now expressed his inner feelings about the situation in Galatia. *First,* he showed concern over them ("I am afraid of you"). They had taken a step in the wrong direction, and he was fearful that they might submit to circumcision. If they did, it would demonstrate that they were not really saved.

*Second,* he was concerned about the results of his missionary effort ("lest I have bestowed upon you labor in vain"). Did they suffer "in vain" (3:4)? Did he work in "vain"? Time would tell. Their response to his letter would determine whether his evangelistic ministry had produced genuine fruit or only

---

[14]Both verbs come from *douleuō*.

leaves. The effect of his labor would be seen in their total acceptance or rejection of the influence of the Judaizers.[15]

## QUESTIONS FOR DISCUSSION

1. How do modern principles of wills and trusts illustrate the concept of spiritual inheritance?
2. What are the modern equivalents of tutors and governors?
3. Could God have become man in any other way than the virgin birth? Can a person who denies the virgin birth be a genuine Christian?
4. Why do some groups insist that a believer receives the Holy Spirit at some point after conversion? How does this belief affect the biblical concept of adoption?
5. Why do Christians behave as though they were spiritual paupers? How can this problem be corrected?
6. Are some evangelicals involved in legalism today? Give illustrations.
7. How can a Christian worker discover whether his work has been in vain? Can this type of failure ever be prevented?

[15]Note the usage of the perfect tense *kekopiaka* ("I have bestowed labor").

# 9

# The Dangers of Legalism
## Galatians 4:12–31

In this section Paul effectively used a double approach to warn the Galatians about the dangers of Judaizing legalism. The first was personal and subjective (4:12–20), and the second was objective and historical (4:21–31).

## I. THE STRAIN BETWEEN PAUL AND THE GALATIANS (4:12–20)

The direct address ("Brethren") served to arrest their attention (cf. 1:11; 3:15; 5:11, 13; 6:1, 18).[1] They were genuine brethren within the family of God, but the false brethren, namely the Judaizing teachers, had caused them to have a strained relationship (2:4). The apostle wanted them to be reconciled to him.

### A. The Warmth of the Past (4:12–15)

In this modern society it does not take much to reduce or to eliminate the loving affection which once existed between newlyweds. Even so, Christians often lose their first love, not only for the Lord, but for each other (Rev. 2:4). When that begins to happen it is very difficult to reverse.

---

[1]The vocative ("brethren") actually occurs in the middle of the verse. The verse begins with the command ("Be").

## 1. He Had Not Been Permanently Hurt (4:12)

He implored the Galatians to identify themselves with him just as he had identified himself with them ("I beseech you, be as I am, for I am as ye are"). He had stood for the uncircumcised Gentile converts both at Jerusalem and at Antioch (2:1, 5, 11). Now it was their turn to stand up for him and for the truth of the gospel in Galatia. He had surrendered his Jewish reputation to become an apostle to the Gentiles. He had become like them to win them to Christ (I Cor. 9:19-22). Out of love he had spoken firmly.

Even though the Galatians had begun to question the apostolic authority and message of Paul, yet he had not turned his back upon them ("ye have not injured me at all"). He hurt inside but he still had his arms extended toward them (4:19). They were his children, for better or for worse (4:19). He could easily say about them, "And I will very gladly spend and be spent for you: though the more abundantly I love you, the less I be loved" (II Cor. 12:15). He did not want them to think that he would hold their disaffection against them.

## 2. He Preached in Weakness (4:13)

He reminded them of his original ministry among them ("at the first"). The Spirit of God had directed Barnabas and him into their region as part of the first aggressive outreach into Gentile territory (Acts 13–14). In fact, he visited their cities twice during that missionary trip. The usage of the singular ("I preached the gospel") is given because Paul was the chief spokesman for the evangelistic team (Acts 14:12). He proclaimed what Christ had revealed to them without any alterations (1:11–12).

He was physically weak when he evangelized them ("through infirmity of the flesh"). The preposition (*dia*) should be translated as "because of" rather than "through."[2] This insight could mean that an infirmity caused him to move into the

---

[2]The preposition *dia* means "because of" when used with the accusative case, and "through" when used with the genitive case. The word *infirmity* is in the accusative case here.

region of Galatia. He may have contacted malaria in the lowlands, and thus he was forced physically to travel into higher elevations. Regardless, it cost him precious physical energy to preach to them. He put himself out to reach them. Had anyone else done this? Had the Judaizers risked their lives? No! They came into Galatia after the hard work had been accomplished. This "infirmity," though unknown, could have been malaria, a severe eye problem (4:15), or the results of persecution, perhaps the effects of stoning (Acts 14:19).

### 3. They Accepted Him Completely (4:14)

How did the Galatians respond to Paul and to his infirmity? *First,* they "despised not" his physical appearance. Quite often men will refuse to listen if a speaker is crippled or ugly or if his voice is marked by harsh tones or stuttering. Leaders are expected to be tall and handsome, but the critics charged that Paul's bodily presence was "weak, and his speech contemptible" (II Cor. 10:10). His body was scarred (II Cor. 11:24–25). Robertson reported, "In the second-century *Acts of Paul and Theda* Paul is pictured as small, short, bow-legged, with eyebrows knit together and an aquiline nose."[3] To the Greek mind this type of appearance was repulsive.

*Second,* they "rejected" not his physical problem. This verb means to spit out, to spurn, or to loathe. It is used of Christ spitting on the ground to make clay for the anointing of the blind man (John 9:6). Tradition states that people would spit at the sight of an epileptic seizure.

*Third,* they "received" him "as an angel of God, even as Christ Jesus." In their pagan superstition they first cried out, "The gods are come down to us in the likeness of men" (Acts 14:11). After conversion they did not treat the apostle as an ordinary man. They saw him as a messenger from heaven and as the personal representative of the Savior.

In retrospect Paul viewed his physical infirmity as a "temptation which was in my flesh."[4] It was divinely ordained so that

---

[3]A. T. Robertson, *Word Pictures in the New Testament,* IV, 254.

[4]Both the NEB and RSV translate it as a temptation to the Galatians to despise Paul.

he might depend more on God's strength (II Cor. 12:9). Paul rejoiced in it and endured it with love (James 1:2, 12).

### 4. They Would Have Given Him Their Eyes (4:15)

In those early days the Galatians had an extreme sense of religious joy. What happened to change all of that? The apostle quizzed them: "Where is then the blessedness ye spake of?" Harrison observed, "They congratulated themselves on being thus favored by an emissary of the Lord."[5] They rejoiced in their salvation, in their deliverance from pagan idolatry, and in their spiritual fellowship with Paul and with one another. In their happiness, they entertained no thoughts that Paul was wrong or that their spiritual experience was less than complete.

Paul apparently had poor eye sight, either congenital, caused by a disease, or inflicted by stoning and frequent beatings. He often used a secretary to compose his books (Rom. 16:22). When he did write he used large letters in this printing (6:11). The Galatians had so much loving gratefulness for him that they would have gladly gone blind if their eyes could have been given to Paul in a transplant operation ("if it had been possible").[6] Paul was the instrument of God to give them spiritual sight, and they would have gladly volunteered their eyes to give Paul the benefit of better physical sight.

## B. The Coldness of the Present (4:16-18)

### 1. They Did Not Like What He Said (4:16)

Their change in attitude toward Paul can be seen in his perplexing question: "Am I therefore become your enemy . . . ?" He went from being an emissary of heaven to being an enemy from hell. The Judaizers had radically changed the feelings of the Galatians toward the apostle.

The reason for the change is seen in the causal clause: " . . .

[5]Everett F. Harrison, *The Wycliffe Bible Commentary,* p. 1293.

[6]Some see this hypothetical impossibility as a symbolic expression of great devotion (Deut. 32:10; Ps. 17:8; Zech. 2:8).

because I tell you the truth."[7] The time of this truthful proclamation is uncertain. *First,* it could refer to the epistle itself because Paul used strong language to describe both the Judaizers and the Galatians (1:6–9; 3:1, 3). Throughout his autobiographical and theological arguments for the doctrine of justification by faith, he used historical and logical evidence. *Second,* it could also refer to the original preaching and teaching of the first journey. At that time they believed that he told the truth. Later when the Judaizers charged that Paul proclaimed a partial gospel, they may have become bitter toward the apostle. After all, if the Judaizers had been right, then faith in Paul's message only would have led them to perdition.

The paradox is that the apostle became their enemy by telling the truth and that the Judaizers became their friends by telling lies. Paul always spoke the truth in love (Eph. 4:15), but they always proclaimed the lie in deceit (II Cor. 11:13–15).

### 2. *They Liked What the Judaizers Said (4:17–18)*

In these verses the concept of religious zeal is mentioned three times ("zealously affect" and "affect"). It involves a deep concern about someone. Closely related to flattery, it is used of courting a person's favor. Based upon motivation, it can be either good or bad. In his evaluation of the ministry of the Judaizers Paul made three crucial statements.

*First,* the false teachers manifested a great concern and interest in the spiritual development of the Galatians ("They zealously affect you"). However, it was not really done for the good of the believers nor for the good of gospel truth ("but not well"). The naive Galatians were impressed with the facade of the heretics. Solomon warned that "the kisses of an enemy are deceitful" (Prov. 27:6).

*Second,* the Judaizers really wanted the Galatians to court the favor of the false teachers ("that ye might affect them"). The heretics wanted the believers both to admire the former and to support them financially (Phil. 3:17–19). They were exploiting the churches. They were in the ministry for what they

---

[7]This is a participle phrase in the Greek (*alētheuōn humin*).

could get out of it. Their means toward the achievement of this goal was the imposition of legalism upon the Galatians ("they would exclude you"). The verb "exclude" (*ekkleisai*) was earlier used of the law which "shut up" sinners (3:23). The Judaizers desired to put up a fence of legalism around the churches and to rule over their new religious prisoners.

*Third,* religious zeal within holiness, truth, and love is always good ("But it is good to be zealously affected always in a good thing"). Paul was not jealous. He did not mind that they could be attracted to other godly teachers. He did not have to be the only one who could communicate truth to them. He rejoiced when they learned from others during his absence ("and not only when I am present with you"). He did oppose, however, the influence of the Judaizers upon them.

## C. The Hope of the Future (4:19–20)

The affectionate address ("my little children") reflects a change of tone within the letter.[8] His earlier appeals manifested the facts that he was a brother ("Brethren") and an apostle ("Galatians") to them. Now he comes as a loving, concerned father. They are still his children regardless of the present alienation. Someone once wrote about the relationship between parents and children:

> When they are little,
> They are a handful;
> When they are grown,
> They are a heartful.

### 1. For Christlikeness in Them (4:19)

Spiritual birth is much like natural birth. A man and a woman come together to bring into being a new life. Even so, God and man cooperate to beget a sinner into the family of God. A believing sinner is begotten both of God (John 1:13; 3:6) and of another Christian (Philem. v. 10). The Galatians were regenerated under the evangelistic ministry of Paul (Acts 13–14). The apostle experienced "birth pains" in those days of out-

---

[8]The word is in the diminutive form (*teknia*).

reach when he appealed to the pagans to turn from idols to the living God.

Now the apostle was having birth pangs all over again because of their spiritual condition ("of whom I travail in birth again"). Some say that the Galatians had lost their salvation under the influence of the Judaizers, and thus he wanted them to be born again twice. If that had been the case, why would he have called them "my little children"? He travailed at the first that Christ might be in them; now he travailed again that Christ might be formed within them ("until Christ be formed in you"). In real life the mother of a prodigal son always agonizes the second time until the erring child returns home. The Galatians needed to grow up and to shape up:

> Till we all come in the unity of the faith, and of the knowledge of the Son of God, unto a perfect man, unto the measure of the stature of the fulness of Christ: That we henceforth be no more children, tossed to and fro, and carried about with every wind of doctrine, by the sleight of men, and cunning craftiness, whereby they lie in wait to deceive (Eph. 4:13–14).

### 2. For Removal of His Doubts (4:20)

Paul wanted to visit them as soon as possible ("I desire to be present with you"). He hoped that his letter would stop their drift toward legalism and their coldness toward him. He desired to talk with them differently than the way in which he had written ("to change my voice").

He admitted that he was perplexed ("for I stand in doubt of you"). He wondered about them and about the actual amount of influence which the Judaizers exercised. How much heresy did they really accept? Were they unwillingly deceived? Were they actually saved? He could only know by their response to his letter and to his next visit.

## II. THE CONFLICT BETWEEN ISAAC AND ISHMAEL (4:21–31)

The characters and events of the Old Testament have often been used as illustrations of New Testament principles. For instance, the Passover lamb was a type of Christ in His sacrificial death (I Cor. 5:7). The essence of faith can be seen in Abel, Enoch, Noah, and others (Heb. 11). A basic law of hermeneutics[9] can be derived from this verse: "Now all these things happened unto them for ensamples [types]: and they are written for our admonition, upon whom the ends of the world are come" (I Cor. 10:11). In this portion of the book Paul planned to use an event out of the life of Abraham to illustrate the principle that a man could not inherit the blessings of the patriarchal covenant through obedience to the law.

## A. The Appeal (4:21)

Someone once said that those who are ignorant of history are bound to repeat it; thus the apostle raised the question: " . . . do ye not hear the law?" Whereas the Judaizers constantly appealed to the moral, civil, and ceremonial regulations of Exodus, Leviticus, and Deuteronomy, Paul pointed to the book of Genesis. Since all of the books were written by Moses, they all constituted *the* Law. To "hear the law" is to read it, to understand it, to believe it, and to obey it (cf. Rev. 2:7).

The command is direct ("Tell me"). He wanted them to answer from the law his question which was taken out of the law. Both the imperative and the question were addressed to "ye that desire to be under the law." The verb ("ye desire to be") shows that the Galatians had not yet submitted to the total bondage of legalism (4:9). They were not yet under the law, but they were willing to be. Their minds and wills had to be corrected immediately.

There is a difference between the phrases "under the law" and "hear the law." The first usage of the noun does not have the article ("the") in the Greek text, but the second has it. The first refers to the principle of legalism, whereas the second specifically points to the law of Moses.

## B. The Historical Situation (4:22-23)

Abraham was seventy-five years old when God made the covenant with him (Gen. 12:4). His wife Sarah was ten years

---

[9]The science studies the laws of biblical interpretation.

younger (Gen. 17:17). At this advanced age he was promised by God that he would have many physical descendants (Gen. 13:16). When no child came after ten years, Sarah encouraged Abraham to have a child by Hagar, her young Egyptian handmaid. Abraham consented, and Ishmael was born when the patriarch was eighty-six years old (Gen. 16:1–16). Later, however, Sarah conceived and bore Isaac when Abraham was one hundred years old (Gen. 21:1–5).

### 1. Two Sons by Two Women (4:22)

The Scriptures alone must be the basis for theological argument; thus the apostle began with an appeal to the infallible Word of God ("For it is written").[10]

Abraham actually had more than two sons. After the death of Sarah, he married Keturah who gave him six more sons (Gen. 25:1–2). However, only "two sons" are important to the illustration of the principle.

Ishmael was born "by a bondmaid." Hagar was a young, fertile girl.[11] She was a slave under the law of Sarah. Sarah, who gave birth to Isaac, was a "freewoman," the rightful wife of Abraham.

### 2. Two Sons by Two Methods (4:23)

Ishmael was born "after the flesh" (cf. 1:11).[12] He was the result of human planning and effort. Abraham believed that he would have children, but when no child was born to Sarah, he heeded the advice of his wife and had a sexual relationship with Hagar. In a sense, Ishmael was born by faith and works. In ancient cultures a childless wife would often give her slave girl as a concubine to her husband.[13] Both Rachel and Leah followed this practice with Jacob (Gen. 30:3, 9). This custom

[10]The perfect tense *gegraptai* is used. What was written stands written. It was authoritative at the time Moses wrote, was still binding in the days of Paul, and is even today.

[11]In the Greek the word *bondmaid* is in the diminutive form (*paidiskēs*). For other usages see Matt. 26:69; Luke 12:45.

[12]Literally "according to flesh" (*kata sarka*).

[13]This practice is attested by the Nuzi tablets and the Babylonian Code of Hammurabi.

was a natural law, but that is just the point that Paul wanted to argue. A man cannot receive the divine promise by a human method.

On the other hand, Isaac was conceived "by promise." It was humanly impossible for Abraham and Sarah to have a child, and they both knew it (Gen. 18:9-13). When they tried to receive the promise through conspiracy and effort they failed. They had to trust God alone for the fulfillment of His pledge. Nothing is too hard for God (Gen. 18:14); thus He "visited Sarah as he had said, and the Lord did unto Sarah as he had spoken" (Gen. 21:1). He brought life out of the deadness of Sarah's womb (Heb. 11:12, 19).

## C. The Allegory (4:24-27)

A biblical "allegory" is a spiritual application of a literal, historical event.[14] It must be distinguished from the liberal theological view that the Bible contains myths. According to this line of thinking, a "myth" is a spiritual truth taken from a biblical event which actually did not occur.[15] Paul firmly believed in the historical accuracy of the events of Genesis.

The following chart shows the blend of the historical and the allegorical into the argument of the apostle

### ABRAHAM

| | |
|---|---|
| Hagar | Sarah |
| Ishmael | Isaac |
| Bondmaid | Freewoman |
| After the flesh | By promise |
| Sinai | Jerusalem |
| Bondage | Free |
| After the flesh | After the Spirit |
| Judaizers | Paul |

[14]The word comes from "another" (*allo*) and "to speak" (*agoreuō*).

[15]For example, the peril of selfishness can be learned from the fall of Adam and Eve, but that pair did not exist in history.

## 1. Birth by Works of the Law (4:24–25)

Sarah and Hagar represented "the two covenants." Sarah became a symbol for the new covenant which internalized the blessings of the Abrahamic covenant (Jer. 31:31–34; Heb. 8:6–7). Hagar became the covenant of law given to Moses on "mount Sinai in Arabia." Just as the birth of Ishmael preceded that of Isaac, so the giving of the law came before the establishment of the new covenant in the blood of Christ, who was the promised seed (3:16).

To be under the law was to be in "bondage." The law demonstrated that men were slaves to sin and that they consequently were under the curse of the law (3:10). Ishmael thus represented the attempt to receive the Abrahamic blessing by the works of the law. Just as Ishmael did not receive the inheritance, so no person can be born again by faith and obedience to the law.

In the first century Hagar also symbolized "Jerusalem which now is." The Jewish people tried to gain the righteousness of God by their own effort: by the sacrificial system centered in the Jerusalem temple, by circumcision, and by conformity to the Mosaic law. This emphasis is exactly what the Judaizers were trying to impose on the Galatians.

Just as Jerusalem was in political bondage to Rome, so the Jewish people ("her children") were in spiritual bondage. They could only be set free by faith in Christ alone.

## 2. Birth by Faith in the Promise (4:26–27)

Sarah corresponds to "Jerusalem which is above." Heavenly Jerusalem is "the city of the living God" (Heb. 12:22; Rev. 21:2). By faith Abraham looked for this city "which hath foundations, whose builder and maker is God" (Heb. 11:10, 16). All genuine believers of all ages are citizens of this place (Phil. 3:20).

This city is "free."[16] A person cannot be set free through birth out of a system of legalistic bondage; thus a sinner could

---

[16]Same word (*eleuthera*) as "freewoman" (4:22), "liberty" (5:1), and "hath made us free" (5:1).

not be delivered out of conformity to the laws of earthly Jerusalem. He must be born out of a free system as Isaac was begotten by Sarah. The opponents of Christ claimed that they were not in bondage because their lives were governed by ritualistic legalism, but the Savior said to them: "If the Son therefore shall make you free, ye shall be free indeed" (John 8:36).

This city is "the mother of us all." The mother of the proper heir, Sarah, represents the system which produces heirs of God through Christ (4:7). Just as God had to quicken the deadness of Sarah's womb, so God must also quicken those who are dead in trespasses and sins (Eph. 2:1). When a person, like Sarah, realizes that he cannot do anything to bring about fulfillment of the divine promise, he will simply trust in the sovereign power of God to save him.

The Old Testament quotation (4:27; cf. Isa. 54:1) looked forward to the future glory and triumph of Israel made possible by the vicarious sufferings of the Messiah (Isa. 53). It also anticipated the salvation of a great host of Gentiles through the atonement of the Savior. In this present church age there are more saved Gentiles than Jews. Israel is "she which hath an husband." Throughout the Scriptures she is known as the wife of Jehovah. The Gentiles are the "barren," "thou that travailest not," and "the desolate."

The Galatians, like Sarah, should rejoice in God's gracious provision of life and redemption through Christ's death and resurrection (6:14). Sarah did not rejoice in the birth of Ishmael, and Paul did not rejoice over the influence of the Judaizers.

## D. The Application (4:28–31)

### 1. In Identity (4:28)

Paul identified himself with the genuine Galatian converts ("we, brethren"). He then proceeded to equate himself and them with Isaac ("as Isaac was"). All of them were "the children of promise." Isaac received the blessing of Abraham because he was begotten of the right mother in the right way. The

Galatian believers and Paul also received the spiritual blessings of covenant because they were regenerated by faith alone in Christ (3:14).

### 2. In Persecution (4:29)

Ishmael was "mocking" Isaac after the latter was weaned (Gen. 21:8–9). If Isaac was about three when this event occurred, then Ishmael was seventeen. The same Hebrew word translated as "mocking" or "laughing" was used elsewhere of the jesting by Lot's prospective sons-in-law (Gen. 19:14), of the accusation against Joseph by the wife of Potiphar (Gen. 39:14), of the actions of the Israelites around the golden calf (Exod. 32:6), and of the jeers of the Philistines toward the blinded Samson (Judg. 16:25). An early Jewish tradition claims that Ishmael was shooting arrows at Isaac.

The closing phrase ("even so it is now") shows the analogy of the two sons to the Galatian situation. The Judaizers, the counterparts of Ishmael, were mocking or persecuting Paul and his associates, the antitypes of Isaac. Just as Ishmael was "born after the flesh," so the Judaizers were born out of legalistic self-effort. Just as Isaac was "born after the Spirit," so were Paul and the genuine believers (John 3:16). The persecution was basically verbal. The Judaizers were making fun of Paul's apostleship and simple message. However, Paul did suffer physically at the hands of unbelieving Jews (5:11; 6:17).

### 3. In Discipline (4:30)

When Sarah saw that Ishmael mocked Isaac, she charged Abraham to cast out of the house both Hagar and her son (Gen. 21:9–10). The reason for the expulsion was that Ishmael would not be a joint heir with Isaac to receive the covenant blessings.[17] Since the sons were born to two different mothers by contrasting means, they could not be equal heirs. In fact, Ishmael was to inherit nothing of the original covenant.

By analogy, Paul wanted the church to excommunicate the

---

[17]The negative "not" in the Greek is very emphatic (*ou mē*). Literally "he shall absolutely, positively not inherit."

Judaizers (Hagar) and the members who accepted the heretical teachings (the sons). Sarah did not tolerate Hagar and Ishmael in her midst, and neither should the church permit the apostates to remain.

### 4. In Summary (4:31)

It is impossible to be born of two mothers. The heir could not be born of both Sarah and Hagar. Even so, spiritual heirs cannot be begotten out of grace and out of works at the same time. The Judaizers claimed that a person had to be saved by both faith and works of legalism. In essence, that concept is impossible. That view actually reduces to salvation by works alone.

Paul knew that both the Galatians and he had been born into the family of God in the right way ("we . . . are of the free"). Like Isaac, they would receive the full inheritance of their spiritual Father.

## QUESTIONS FOR DISCUSSION

1. Are Christians too sensitive to criticisms of their character and work? Do they react rather than act in difficult situations?
2. Are Christians too impressed with the physical appearances of pulpit candidates? Do they look down on those who are infirmed or crippled?
3. Should Christians donate key organs of their body to others? To medical schools?
4. Why are some Christians easily influenced by persuasive false teachers? What can be done to prevent immature believers from falling into error? From supporting financially false groups?
5. When do parents have more concern for their children? In the early years? In the later years? Should they be concerned at all times?
6. Are enough sermons preached out of the Old Testament? How can believers properly apply these Scriptures to contemporary living?
7. Are churches afraid to exercise discipline today? In doctrinal issues? In moral problems?

# 10

# The Appeal to Liberty and Love
## Galatians 5:1 −15

The oppressed of one revolution often became the oppressors of the next. Those who argue for freedom for themselves can sometimes be reluctant to give it to others. The Russian people simply exchanged one form of slavery for another when they overthrew the Czar for communism. Revolutions can be either good or bad. More times than not, they lead to anarchy and hatred rather than to liberty and love.

The Judaizers charged that the teaching of Paul would lead the Galatians into lawlessness. The apostle countered that the heretics wanted to replace one expression of legalistic bondage for another. Who was right? The churches were confused. In this section Paul argued that a proper apprehension of the doctrine of justification by grace through faith alone would lead to a life of spiritual freedom and holy love.

## I. STAND IN LIBERTY (5:1-12)

After the Civil War a great majority of the slaves became sharecroppers. Although they were free, they did not enjoy their freedom. In some cases they were worse off than before. Under the influence of the Judaizers, the Galatians were beginning to find themselves in a similar situation. Set free by the great emancipator of the soul, Jesus Christ, they soon were acquiescing to the demands of the legalists. The apostle wanted them to take a stand, to act like free men, not like slaves.

## A. The Command to Stedfastness (5:1)

Two commands were given. The first was positive; the second was negative.

### 1. Stand in Liberty (5:1a)

The force behind the command ("stand") is to take a decisive action. The word literally means "Take a stand and keep on standing."[1] They were to take a firm position of orthodoxy within the doctrine of salvation. Some had wilted under the constant barrages of the Judaizers, whereas others had surrendered. In this holy war he wanted them to stand against satanic deception (Eph. 6:11, 14) and to stand fast in the faith (I Cor. 16:13). He wanted no retreats.

Although the imperative has grammatical strength, it actually occurs in the middle of the sentence. The real emphasis lies in the means or sphere of the stand, namely "liberty." The proper word order is: "In [by] the liberty by which Christ set us free, stand." The aspect of freedom or liberty has been the central theme of this context (4:22, 23, 26, 30, 31).[2]

Three characteristics of this liberty are enumerated. *First,* it is specific (note the usage of "the"). A believer has no obligation to any system of legalism which is required for justification or sanctification. He is "not under the law, but under grace" (Rom. 6:14). However, he is always under the moral law of God (I Cor. 9:21), the laws of the family (Eph. 5:22—6:9), and the laws of government (Rom. 13:1-7).

*Second,* it is a liberty achieved only by Christ through His death and resurrection. Only He could say, "If the Son therefore shall make you free, ye shall be free indeed" (John 8:36). He did not set men free from the bondage of the law and the penalty of sin in order that they might keep on sinning. He delivered sinners so that they might be free to please God, not that they might please themselves (Rom. 15:1-3). When He

---

[1] It is in the perfect tense (*stēkete*).

[2] The two words *freedom* and *liberty* are used synonymously and come from the same Greek stem (*eleutheroō*).

146

died He was "blotting out the handwriting of ordinances that was against us, which was contrary to us, and took it out of the way, nailing it to his cross" (Col. 2:14).

*Third,* it takes place at conversion. The verb ("hath made free") points to an accomplished, past event.[3] Provisionally it occurred at the cross, but practically it happened at the regeneration of the sinner. The shackles of sin and selfishness were removed. The power of the gravitational pull of the sin nature downward has been conquered. The believer is now free to become and to do all that God in His wisdom wanted men to be. He can now become a totally functioning human being in body, soul, and spirit.

## 2. Do Not Be Entangled with Legalism (5:1b)

The negative command translates, "Stop becoming entangled with."[4] The Galatians who were permitting themselves to get involved in legalistic practices had to cease. The verb "entangled" (*enechesthe*) was used of trappers who put out snares to catch their prey. Solomon said, "A man that flattereth his neighbor spreadeth a net for his feet" (Prov. 29:5). The Judaizers, through their hypocritical compliments, were trying to make victims out of the Galatians (4:17). The believers had to extricate themselves before it was too late.

The "yoke of bondage" is the Mosaic law. As a "yoke," it restricted men. Since men broke the commandments, they were under the "bondage" of the curse. At the council of Jerusalem Peter declared, "Now therefore why tempt ye God, to put a yoke upon the neck of the disciples, which neither our fathers nor we were able to bear" (Acts. 15:10). The apostles and elders agreed that both Gentile and Jewish believers are not under the law. In this age Christians should voluntarily take the yoke of Christ upon themselves, for His yoke is "easy" and His burden is "light" (Matt. 11:29–30). The Mosaic law was oppressive, but a life lived in the will of God is liberating.

[3]It is the aorist tense (*ēleutherōse*).

[4]The usage of *mē* with the present imperative (*enechesthe*) means to stop doing what you are doing.

The adverb ("again") shows that in their unsaved experiences they were involved in legalism, either within paganism or Judaism (4:8–9).

## B. The Problems of Mixing Law and Grace (5:2–4)

### 1. No Profit from Christ (5:2)

Whenever the apostle wanted to make a strong, personal assertion, he would begin with the words: "I Paul" (cf. II Cor. 10:1; Eph. 3:1). The addition of the exclamatory imperative ("Behold") further strengthens the seriousness of the following remarks.

The conditional protasis ("if ye be circumcised") shows that the Galatians had not yet submitted to the rite. Paul was not against circumcision *per se*. For the sake of a more effective testimony to the Jews, he had Timothy circumcised (Acts 16:3), and this event occurred in Galatia. He did not advocate the end of circumcision as part of the Jewish religious heritage (Acts 21:21). Rather he argued that circumcision was not necessary for salvation, either for the Jew or the Gentile:

> Is any man called being uncircumcised? let him not become uncircumcised. Is any man called in uncircumcision? let him not be circumcised. Circumcision is nothing, and uncircumcision is nothing, but the keeping of the commandments of God (I Cor. 7:18–19).

The concluding apodosis ("Christ shall profit you nothing") declares that no merit of the Savior's death and resurrection would be reckoned to the account of any person who believed that circumcision was essential for justification. A man is not saved by faith in what Christ has done *and* by faith in what he can do, whether that involves circumcision, baptism, or any other sacramental work. When some deed is added as a requirement for heaven, that action demonstrates that the person has not exercised the type of faith which the Bible demands. Saving faith trusts Christ only and repudiates any attempt of man to produce a meritorious work. Paul warned that if anyone received circumcision as an additional means of salvation he would manifest that he was really an unsaved person.

A threshing floor near Konya, Turkey (site of ancient Iconium).

149

## 2. *Debtor to the Whole Law (5:3)*

Another strong affirmation is made here ("For I testify again"). The issue of legal justification was not academic nor did Paul and the Judaizers use two different methods to achieve the same goal. At issue was the very essence of the gospel message: Is salvation of the Lord or is it of man?

The charge was given "to every man that is circumcised." The concept behind the verb (*peritemnomenōi*)[5] points to those who were about to be circumcised, not to those who had already submitted to the rite, although the principle would apply to both groups.

To Paul circumcision was the first step into a life of bondage under legalism (2:3-4). If a person accepted the rite as necessary to salvation, he became "a debtor to do the whole law." Earlier it was pointed out that a person must keep all of the law all of the time to gain heaven. If he breaks just one law once, then he falls under the curse of the law (3:10). On the basis of legalism there is no reason why faith in Christ is even required. It is negated by the obligation of human effort (2:21).

## 3. *Fallen from Grace (5:4)*

The remarks of this verse are given to a specific group ("whosoever of you are justified by the law"). This would include the Judaizers and their converts. The issue at stake was justification, not sanctification. The present tense of the verb reads, "are being justified" (*dikaiousthe*). Within legalism, justification is an on-going process. It is never achieved before death. A person can never attain a justified position because he must continually obey all of the laws all of the time. He can never rest in what he has done or in what someone else has done because there is always more to do.

Two verbal ideas characterize this group. *First,* "Christ is become of no effect unto you." The Greek text literally reads, "You were rendered null and void away from Christ."[6] The

[5]Present passive participle.

[6]The second person plural verb is used (*katērgēthēte*). The pronoun "whosoever" (*hoitines*) is nominative plural.

meritorious value of Christ's person and redemptive work has been rendered inoperative within the life of a person who is trying to work his way into heaven. The person thus is not in Christ, nor is Christ in him. He is apart from the Savior, devoid of the righteousness of God which is imputed by faith alone.

*Second,* they are "fallen from grace." This phrase has been greatly misinterpreted and misapplied. It does not refer to the losing of personal salvation. No great moral sin is under discussion here. This is a doctrinal matter. The issue is How is a person justified? not Can a justified person lose his salvation? A contrast exists between justification by grace and justification by law. When a person believes that circumcision and law keeping are essential for salvation, then he has fallen from the divine standard of justification (grace) to the human means (law). Such a fall demonstrates his lack of salvation, not his loss of it. Salvation is by grace through faith apart from works (Eph. 2:8–9). It is gained and maintained by grace alone (Rom. 5:1–2).

## C. The Privileges of Believers (5:5–6)

### 1. Hope of Righteousness (5:5)

They have an eager anticipation of the future. The verb "wait" (*apekdechometha*) literally means "to receive from out of." When Christ comes out of heaven to translate the living and to raise the dead, the believer will receive from Him the completion of salvation, namely an immortal, incorruptible body.

They await "the hope of righteousness." They are not waiting for righteousness; rather they have righteousness which gives them hope for the future. A genuine believer is marked by "hope" (I Cor. 13:13; I Thess. 1:3). Paul wrote elsewhere:

> For we are saved by hope: but hope that is seen is not hope: for what a man seeth, why doth he yet hope for? But if we hope for that we see not, then do we with patience wait for it (Rom. 8:24–25).

Kent claims that the "hope" is "the expectation of the final public acknowledgement by God of the believer's acceptability with him."[7]

This hope is made possible "through the Spirit . . . by faith."[8] The presence of the Spirit within the life guarantees the acceptance of the child of God and verifies the validity of his faith (4:6). The apostle also said:

> . . . but the Spirit is life because of righteousness. But if the Spirit of him that raised up Jesus from the dead dwell in you, he that raised up Christ from the dead shall also quicken your mortal bodies by his Spirit that dwelleth in you (Rom. 8:10–11).

Legalism has never delivered one man from the penalty of spiritual death and the problem of physical death, but faith in the crucified, resurrected Christ has achieved both. Instead of worrying and working, the believer can look forward to all that God has promised.

### 2. Equality in Christ (5:6a)

In Christ there is spiritual oneness (3:28). A circumcised Jew who gets saved has no advantage over an uncircumcised Gentile who becomes a Christian, and the reverse situation is also true. Thus circumcision is not essential for justification or sanctification.

### 3. Works of Faith Through Love (5:6b)

What does count to God and to Paul is "faith which worketh by love." Faith "availeth" (ischuei); it is strong and it has an innate ability to produce holy deeds. It is not abstract, intellectual, cold, barren, or lifeless.

The faith which saves has energy to work ("worketh").[9] The Judaizers claimed that works were essential for salvation, but Paul charged that works were the evidence of saving faith. The

[7]Homer A. Kent, Jr., *The Freedom of God's Sons*, p. 145.

[8]Although separated in the English, they appear together in the Greek text: *pneumati ek pisteōs*.

[9]The English word *energy* comes from this Greek term (*energoumenē*).

grace of God which saves men also teaches them to deny sin and to live holy lives (Titus 2:11-14). All genuine believers will be "zealous of good works" (Titus 2:14; 3:8).

The motivation for the works of faith is "love." A genuine believer will work not to gain or to keep salvation, but rather to show his loving gratitude for all that Christ has done for him. The "love of Christ constraineth" him (II Cor. 5:14). Divine love must be returned by human love (I John 4:19).

## D. The Perils of the False Teachers (5:7-12)

### 1. They Hinder You (5:7)

Under the leadership of Paul and their elders, the Galatians were continuing in the faith (Acts 14:22-23). The apostle equated their spiritual progress with the running of a race ("ye did run well"). They had started, they were running, but they had not yet finished.[10] They had begun in the Spirit and they were proceeding in the Spirit (3:3; 5:16). They were running with faith and patience as they looked to Jesus, the author and finisher of their faith (Heb. 12:1-2). Like Paul, they tried to run with purpose and excellence (I Cor. 9:24-26). According to Judaism, no orthodox Jew could or would run in the Greek games because it involved nudity and worship of the heathen gods; however, this race was obligatory upon both Jewish and Gentile believers.

Quite often in races, a runner will suddenly dart in front of another, causing the second athlete to break stride, to stumble, or to be pushed off the track. Spiritually, this happened to the Galatians. The question ("who did hinder you") shows that someone had cut in front of them causing them to fall or to stumble.[11] Although many false teachers troubled the church (1:7), the emphasis here is on the leader of the Judaizers.[12]

The result of the interference was disobedience to the truth ("that ye should not obey the truth"). They were now trying to

[10]The verb is in the imperfect tense (*etrechete*): "Ye were running."
[11]The literal meaning of "hinder" (*anekopse*) is "to cut in front of."
[12]The interrogative pronoun "who" (*tis*) is singular.

finish the race by legalism and self rather than by faith and the Spirit.

### 2. They Persuade You (5:8)

Three words in this section are related: "obey" (5:7), "persuasion" (5:8), and "have confidence" (5:10).[13] In a sense, there is a play on words here. The "persuasion" not to have persuasion with respect to the truth of grace had been imposed upon them.

This change of conviction did not have its source in God ("not of him that calleth you"). God had called them into the grace of Christ, and now they were being moved toward a false gospel (1:6). God doesn't call men to Himself by two different systems of salvation. He is "one God, which shall justify the circumcision by faith, and uncircumcision through faith" (Rom. 3:30).

The false persuasion, of course, came from the Judaizers, the ministers of Satan (II Cor. 11:13–15). Paul saw beyond the human opponent to the supernatural enemy. Satan was attacking God through the hostility of the Judaizers toward the apostle. On another occasion Satan used unbelieving Jews to hinder Paul's return to Thessalonica (I Thess. 2:14–16; cf. 2:18).

### 3. They Permeate You (5:9)

A familiar axiom was quoted to show the subtle, corrupting influence of the Judaizers in their midst: "A little leaven leaveneth the whole lump." The nature of leaven is to spread until the whole is affected; it is not content with just a part. The nature of cancerous cells within a human body is the same. Moral and doctrinal error, like yeast and cancer, will spread undetected. The only remedy is vigilance, followed by immediate purging or surgery. In a similar situation where error had been tolerated to the spiritual detriment of the congregation, Paul commanded: "Purge out therefore the old leaven, that ye may be a new lump" (I Cor. 5:7). The church had to expel the Judaizers if it expected to be healthy again.

No amount of heresy should ever be permitted to exist

---

[13]They are all based upon the Greek stem *peithō*.

within a local church. It only takes a "little" sin to begin the leavening process. At Galatia they were already observing a legalistic calendar (4:10).

### 4. *They Trouble You (5:10)*

This verse centers around the three key principals within the book: Paul ("I"), the Galatians ("ye"), and the Judaizer ("he"). *First,* Paul stated his conviction that the believers would recognize the doctrinal peril, that they would reject legalism for a life of faith, and that they would expel the heretics ("I have confidence"). He firmly believed that they would ultimately obey what he had taught and written. This inner persuasion was not wishful thinking, but an attitude of heart instilled "through the Lord."

*Second,* the church would get its thinking straightened out ("that ye will be otherwise minded"). Just as Satan had deceived Eve, their minds were being "corrupted from the simplicity that is in Christ" (II Cor. 11:3). This trend in thinking would be reversed.

*Third,* the leader of the Judaizers would receive judgment both from the church and God ("he that troubleth you shall bear his judgment"). The singular ("he") refers to the principal heretical teacher, although the entire group was actually causing trouble (1:7). The trouble was both mental and spiritual, involving the perversion of the gospel. The identity of this leader was unknown to Paul ("whosoever he be"), but this did not matter, because the problem was really an issue of principle, not personality. Regardless of the man's reputation or influence, he deserved to be judged.

### 5. *They Persecute Paul (5:11)*

The Judaizers claimed that Paul was a "religious chameleon." They charged that Paul preached the necessity of circumcision to a Jewish audience but that he omitted that requirement for salvation when he spoke to a Gentile congregation. The apostle, of course, never did what they said, and he denied the accusation vehemently.

For the sake of argument, he assumed the reality of their

claim ("if I yet preach circumcision").[14] The usage of the adverb ("yet" or "still") shows that he did preach the necessity of circumcision during his pharisaical life.

Two results of the assumption are then given. *First,* there would have been no persecution if the Judaizers had been right. The perceptive question ("Why do I yet suffer persecution?") reveals the inconsistency of the charge. Throughout Paul's travels, his persecutors had largely been Jews, not Gentiles. He was constantly being kicked out of synagogues. The opposite would have been true if the Judaizers had been right.

*Second,* the "offence of the cross" would have been rendered inoperative by his preaching of circumcision. The "offence" or "scandal" (*skandalon*) of the cross includes the total helplessness of man to contribute to his salvation. It destroys the wisdom and power of men (I Cor. 1:18–25). Contrariwise the Judaizers were afraid to accept the offence of the cross because they disliked persecution themselves (6:12).

### 6. They Unsettle You (5:12)

The Judaizers caused further "trouble." This verb (*anastatatountes*) means to unsettle or to drive someone from his house.[15] In a sense, the heretics were evicting the Galatians from the house of grace built upon the rock foundation of Christ and were trying to move them into the house of self-righteous works (cf. Matt. 7:24–27).

Paul wished that these troublemakers might be "cut off" (*apokopsontai*). There is holy sarcasm behind his meaning. The Judaizers, of course, used knives to cut off the foreskin in the rite of circumcision. Some believe that the apostle wanted them to "mutilate themselves."[16] If they castrated themselves, they would not be able to produce new converts. Or it may be a descriptive metaphor to reinforce his request for their physical removal from the Galatian churches.

---

[14]The conditional protasis uses *ei* with the present indicative *kērussō.*

[15]The earlier word used for "trouble" was *tarassō* (1:7; 5:10).

[16]The RSV renders the verb this way, seeing it as a reflexive middle.

## II. STAND IN LOVE (5:13-15)

The mark of genuine spiritual discipleship is love (John 13:35). What is the cause of such love? Legalism or liberty in Christ?

### A. Basis of Love (5:13)

Wiersbe says that liberty minus love will issue in license, whereas liberty plus love will result in service.[17]

#### 1. Liberty Without Love (5:13a)

All believers "have been called unto liberty." This is the efficacious call to salvation (1:6; 5:8; Rom. 8:28, 30). The result of this call is a justified position before God (Rom. 8:30). The basis of the call is "liberty." The preposition "unto" (*epi*) is normally translated as "upon." The call of God rests upon liberty, not bondage.

What is the purpose of this liberty? It should not be used as "an occasion to the flesh." Licentiousness and liberty are not synonymous. The "flesh" refers to the sin nature which is still an integral part of the redeemed sinner. Believers are not to use their freedom from the Mosaic law to be morally lawless. The word *occasion* (*aphormēn*) means a starting point, a base of operations, or a springboard for action.

#### 2. Liberty to Love (5:13b)

Using liberty for selfish pursuits is lust, not love. The real goal of spiritual liberty is to "serve one another."[18] A sinner has been set free from the bondage of self, sin, and Satan so that he might become a slave to others.

He has become a slave under the law of love ("by love"). Service without love becomes a punishment, but service through love becomes a blessing to all. He is now free to love God, others, and self without sinful restrictions.

---

[17]Warren W. Wiersbe, *Be Free,* p. 127.

[18]The verb "serve" is an imperative (*douleuete*). The word *slave* (*doulos*) is based upon this verb.

## B. Options of Love (5:14-15)

### 1. Presence of Love (5:14)

The Judaizers failed to see beyond the precepts of the law to its principle. The essence of the law could be summarized "in one word": *love*. If a person really loved God, he would not violate the commandments of the first table. He would not worship images or false gods, would not take God's name in vain, and he would observe a day of worship (Exod. 20:1-11). If a person really loved his neighbor as himself, he would honor his parents, would not kill his neighbor, and would not steal his wife, property, or reputation (Exod. 20:12-17). Elsewhere Paul wrote, "Love worketh no ill to his neighbor: therefore love is the fulfilling of the law" (Rom. 13:10; cf. Lev. 19:18). In this age the believer is not under the specific precepts of the law, but he must always be under the principle of love which permeated the Mosaic law.

### 2. Absence of Love (5:15)

The conditional protasis stated what was actually going on in the churches ("But if ye bite and devour one another").[19] The legalism of the Judaizers and the misuse of liberty combined to produce an atmosphere of destructive criticism. Instead of serving each other, Christians were being served as food for gossip. They became Christian cannibals!

Paul then issued a warning: "Take heed that ye be not consumed one of another." James and John wanted to bring down heavenly fire to consume the Samaritan opponents of Christ, but He rebuked them: "Ye know not what manner of spirit ye are of" (Luke 9:55). Christ came to save lives, not to destroy them (Luke 9:56). In the defense of the gospel Christians must "contend for the faith" without being contentious (Jude v. 3). They must always speak the truth in love (Eph. 4:15). They must always "overcome evil with good" (Rom. 12:21).

Reciprocal criticism always leads to reciprocal destruction.

---

[19]The conditional particle "if" (ei) with the two indicative verbs is used to state a present reality.

There is an apocryphal story of two snakes that grabbed each other by the tail and subsequently swallowed each other.[20] Much too often Christians are guilty of similar behavior.

## QUESTIONS FOR DISCUSSION

1. What different kinds of liberty exist in the world today? In what ways do they illustrate spiritual freedom?
2. How can people become entangled in the bondage of legalism today? Are most Christians too legalistic? Why?
3. Why do people equate "falling from grace" with the loss of salvation? Does the majority of Christians believe in eternal security?
4. Do some Christians think that they are better than others because of their past religious and cultural backgrounds? How can their thinking be changed?
5. Who are the modern Judaizers? How do they gain access into the churches?
6. Do Christians understand the principles of grace? Are they afraid to trust others with liberty? Why?
7. Are church splits ever justified? Why can't Christians get along with each other?

[20]A. T. Robertson, *Word Pictures in the New Testament,* IV, 311.

# 11

# *The Basis of Sanctification*
### *Galatians 5:16–23*

Just as justification is not possible through the efforts of self, so sanctification cannot be achieved through one's own energy either. Both come from the provision and power of God.

The basic meaning of "sanctify" (*hagiazō*) is "to set apart." There are four stages within the biblical concept of sanctification. *First, preparatory* sanctification is that activity of the Holy Spirit whereby He quickens within the sinner a need of salvation (II Thess. 2:13). *Second, positional* sanctification occurs at the moment of conversion so that the believing sinner is eternally set apart unto God as His possession (I Cor. 6:11; Heb. 10:14). This action turns sinners into saints (I Cor. 1:2). *Third, progressive* sanctification is that work of the triune God whereby He sets apart the Christian unto Himself from the temptations of the world, the flesh, and the devil (John 17:17; Eph. 5:26). This happens during the entire lifetime of the believer on earth and is achieved by his yieldedness to the Spirit and his obedience to the Scriptures. *Fourth, prospective* sanctification occurs either at physical death or at the return of Christ, resulting in a total separation from the sin nature and its effects. In this sense, it is the equivalent of glorification (Rom. 8:30).

Paul wanted the Galatians to realize that obedience to the law was not necessary for progressive sanctification. The sinner is not only justified by faith, but he is also sanctified by faith (Rom. 1:17).

# I. THE NATURE OF SPIRITUALITY (5:16-18)

What is spirituality? Who is spiritual? Is it accomplished by legalistic conformity, either to the Mosaic law or to a denominational list of dos and don'ts? What part does the Holy Spirit have? The self?

## A. Its Command (5:16)

### 1. The Definition (5:16a)

The command is direct and simple: "Walk in the Spirit."[1] Someone has said that a pilgrimage of a thousand miles begins with a single step. So it is with spirituality. It is not achieved, once and for all, in an instantaneous event; rather it is a progressive, lifelong pursuit.

The imperative can also be translated, "Keep on walking."[2] In contrast to running, walking is slower; it involves time and persistence. In contrast to sitting, walking needs initiative and purpose. To be spiritual a Christian must obey the command. Unfortunately some have refused.

The concept of walking is an apt description of the Christian life. It should be a natural, outward manifestation of the supernatural life which is within him. Most people have a distinctive walk in ordinary life: they bounce, sway, or lean. Likewise a believer should be marked by his walk. He should walk worthy of the divine calling in all humility (Eph. 4:1), should walk unlike the unsaved (Eph. 4:17), should walk in sacrificial love (Eph. 5:2), should walk as a child of light (Eph. 5:8), and should walk circumspectly (Eph. 5:15).

The above requirements of the Christian walk must be done by means of the Holy Spirit. The verse shows this emphasis: "By the Spirit walk."[3] He must walk in the realm of the Spirit, under His control, and totally dependent on Him. A fish has the freedom to act like a fish only as it moves within water.

[1] In the Greek, it is only two words: *pneumati peripateite*.

[2] It is a present imperative.

[3] The word *Spirit* (*pneumati*) occurs first. It can be regarded as a locative of sphere or an instrumental of means.

Dependent on that environment, it ceases to function properly when removed from that habitat. So it is with the child of God. He can only act as a spiritual Christian while he is living under the influence of the Spirit. The Spirit must become the environment and the means by which the Christian exercises his liberty in Christ. Just as the fish glides through the water, so the walk of a spiritual Christian should appear to be effortless.

Three characteristics will mark the spiritual walk. *First,* the believer will not grieve the Holy Spirit (Eph. 4:30). The Spirit is grieved when a believer deliberately, persistently sins against his fellow Christians (Eph. 4:25–32). Conversely he must confess and forsake these sins. *Second,* he will not quench the Spirit (I Thess. 5:19). He quenches the Spirit when he refuses to permit the Spirit to express Himself through his life. In other words, he is not yielded, stamping out the divine fire within Him. *Third,* he will be filled with the Spirit (Eph. 5:18). This does not mean that he gets more of the Holy Spirit, but only that the Spirit gets more of him. The Spirit infuses his very being from within causing him to act strangely in the eyes of a nonspiritual world (I Peter 4:4). In a sense, he has become a "spiritual drunk" (Eph. 5:18), marked by joy, thanksgiving, and submission (Eph. 5:19–21).

### 2. The Result (5:16b)

The result of constant obedience to the command is guaranteed: ". . . and ye shall not fulfil the lust of the flesh." The negative is very emphatic: "You shall absolutely, positively not fulfil."[4] There is no exception. Victory over the possibility of daily sin comes from complete surrender to the Holy Spirit, not from conformity to a legalistic code.

The "flesh" refers to the sin principle which operates through man's human nature. It functions through the mind, the will, the emotions, and the physical organs. The "lust of the flesh," then, incorporates all of the evil desires that originate within fallen human nature. They must be distinguished from

---

[4]The emphatic double negative (*ou mē*) is used.

those allurements which stem from Satan and the world, although these two make their appeal to man's baser self.

A spiritual believer is not promised relief from temptation, but he will be delivered from the fulfillment of those temptations. Christ is the perfect example. He constantly walked in the Spirit and never sinned. Although He was tempted, He never responded because He was totally submissive to the will of God expressed in Scripture.

## B. Its Conflict (5:17)

A Christian is a creature of two environments. Unlike the fish whose one nature is adaptable to only one habitat, the believer can function within two realms.

### 1. He Has Two Natures

Before Adam sinned he had a perfect human nature with a will disposed toward God. After he sinned he still had a human nature, but his will was not oriented toward self and sin. In his fall he thus obtained a sin nature. He became a sinful man, and all those who have been born into the human race have inherited both a human nature and a sin nature from their parents.

At conversion the sinful man becomes a partaker of the divine nature (II Peter 1:4). The seed of God is now in him (I Peter 1:23; I John 3:9). Thus the Christian is a human being who has two natures within him. In this passage the titles for the sin nature ("the flesh") and the divine nature ("the Spirit") are given. They are elsewhere distinguished as "the old man, which is corrupt according to the deceitful lusts" (Eph. 4:22) and "the new man, which after God is created in righteousness and true holiness" (Eph. 4:24). What Adam lost through his sin, the sinner can regain through redemption.

At death the Christian will get rid of his sin nature but he will forever remain human and a child of God. At the resurrection he will get a new immortal, incorruptible body but not a new humanity.

### 2. *He Has Two Desires*

The two natures are diametrically opposed to each other ("these are contrary the one to the other"). Although both work in and through the human nature of the Christian (his intelligence, emotion, and will), they are exclusive of each other. The new divine nature was not implanted to improve or to displace the old sin nature, and neither can the sin nature pollute the holy divine nature. They are two separate entities. A Christian, thus, is a spiritual paradox. He is both a sinner and a child of God. This fact alone causes the angels to investigate the essence of human salvation (I Peter 1:12).

Both natures "lust." The verb (*epithumei*) connotes an intense desire, which can be either holy or evil, based upon source, motivation, and object. Paul desired to return to Thessalonica and later to be with Christ (I Thess. 2:17; Phil. 1:23). These were noble aspirations.

When the flesh lusts it has both an unholy source and goal. It seeks to use the will of man for wicked thoughts and deeds. In so doing, it opposes ("against") the presence of the Spirit within the believer. On the other hand, when the Spirit lusts, He desires the Christian to be yielded to Him. The flesh and the Spirit are enemies in the same sense that God and Satan are foes. They are in conflict with each other, not with the man himself.

### 3. *He Has Perplexity*

This inner struggle is the cause of spiritual frustration and defeat for many. The connective ("so that," *hina*) shows the purpose or result of that conflict. It means that "ye cannot do the things that ye would". The contrast here is between willing and doing. The willing comes out of the human will (human nature), but it is affected by the two natures ("flesh" or "Spirit"). The believer may will to do the lusts of the flesh, but the Spirit will prevent him from consistent sinning (I John 3:6, 8–9). Contrariwise he may will to obey the Spirit, but the flesh will restrict him. Herein lies the dilemma. How can the Christian be holy when he still has a sin nature?

Before Paul learned the secret of victory, he confessed to the same inner struggle:

> For that which I do I allow not: for what I would, that do I not; but what I hate, that do I. If then I do that which I would not, I consent unto the law that it is good. Now then it is no more I that do it, but sin that dwelleth in me. For I know that in me (that is, in my flesh,) dwelleth no good thing: for to will is present with me; but how to perform that which is good I find not. For the good that I would I do not: but the evil which I would not, that I do. Now if I do that I would not, it is no more I that do it, but sin that dwelleth in me. I find then a law, that, when I would do good, evil is present with me. For I delight in the law of God after the inward man: But I see another law in my members, warring against the law of my mind, and bringing me into captivity to the law of sin which is in my members (Rom. 7:15-23).

All Christians can sympathize with his conclusion: "O wretched man that I am! who shall deliver me from the body of this death?" (Rom. 7:24).

Why is victory so difficult to achieve? In the above passage, note the constant reference to the self ("I"). A person cannot just *will* to overcome the flesh. The will, in itself, does not provide the ability to do. The power to be holy comes only from God; thus, he must surrender his will in cleanliness to the Spirit who will produce through him practical righteousness.

## C. Its Solution (5:18)

Paul assumed that the Galatians were Spirit-directed for the most part ("But if ye be led of the Spirit").[5] If a believer is being led by the Spirit, then he is not under the constant, conscious pressure of legalism, whether imposed by others or by self. This question does not give him anxiety: Should I do this, or that? Instead he does what is natural for him to do, and what is natural is spiritual, because he is controlled by the Spirit.

The Spirit of God cannot perform His sanctifying work while

[5]The protasis uses ei ("if") with the present indicative. This usage assumes reality.

a person is trying to become spiritual through conformity to a set of laws. The Spirit can lead only when a person sees himself set free from the law and placed under grace. Unfortunately legalistic conformity and spirituality have been equated in many circles; however, this position reflects phariseeism more than Christlikeness.

The law, in fact, was the instrument through which the human nature manifested its moral weakness. Paul wrote:

> For what the law could not do, in that it was weak through the flesh, God sending his own Son in the likeness of sinful flesh, and for sin, condemned sin in the flesh: That the righteousness of the law might be fulfilled in us, who walk not after the flesh, but after the Spirit (Rom. 8:3–4).

The paradox is that the righteousness of the law is achieved by freedom from the law through the dynamic ministry of the Spirit within the believer.

## II. THE CONTRAST BETWEEN WORKS AND FRUIT
### (5:19–23)

Earlier there was a clash between the flesh and the Spirit. Now a contrast is established between "the works of the flesh" and "the fruit of the Spirit."

### A. The Works of the Flesh (5:19–21)

If a believer does not walk in the Spirit, he will fulfill the lust of the flesh (5:16). That fulfillment is also called a work of the flesh. Since the Christian has the same sin nature which he possessed in his unsaved life, he is therefore capable of thinking and doing the same sins if he is not yielded to the indwelling Spirit. When that occurs, he then is a carnal believer, controlled by the flesh and walking as an unsaved man (Rom. 8:5–6; I Cor. 3:3).

Here seventeen works of the flesh are manifest, both to God

and to man. They cannot be hidden.[6] There are more ("and such like"), of course, but these were sufficient to describe the outward expression of the sinful flesh. They seem to divide into four major categories.

### 1. Sexual Sins (5:19)

Four are mentioned. *Adultery (moicheia)* refers to premarital and extramarital sexual intercourse. It can be committed by both the married and the unmarried. In contexts which mention both "adultery" and "fornication," it usually points to the sensual sins of a married person. It was condemned in the Ten Commandments (Exod. 20:14). Jesus extended the sin from its activity to its attitude: "But I say unto you, that whosoever looketh on a woman to lust after her hath committed adultery with her already in his heart" (Matt. 5:28).

*Fornication (porneia)* is the general word used for any sexual sin. It is used of the prostitute or the harlot (James 2:25; Rev. 17:1, 5). When connected with adultery, it embraces normally the sensual sins of the unmarried. The English word *pornography* is based on the Greek term.

*Uncleanness* is moral impurity. It is marked by a filthy mind, full of sensually suggestive thoughts and humor (Eph. 5:3–4). It reads illicit sex even into the most wholesome situations. Marked by perverted fantasies, it is expressed through pornographic literature and movies.

*Lasciviousness* is such moral wantonness that it even offends public decency. In many situations, it could include both homosexuality and lesbianism. It contains lewdness (Rom. 13:13; II Cor. 12:21).

### 2. Religious Sins (5:20a)

Two are cited. *Idolatry,* widespread in the first century, involved the worship of pagan deities through idols; however, the people unwittingly were serving demons (I Cor. 10:19–20). Since it is mentioned right after the sexual sins, it could also

---

[6]The predicate adjective "manifest" is emphatic, appearing first in the sentence.

include the practice of having illicit sexual relationships with the temple priests and priestesses.[7]

*Witchcraft* embraced astrology, the magical arts, and demonic spiritism. The word *pharmacy* comes from the Greek term (*pharmakeia*). Thus this sin could utilize drugs to create religious trances and hypnosis. Very prominent in neighboring Ephesus (Acts 19:19), it will be a major sin during the great tribulation when the Antichrist will exercise his power (Rev. 9:21; 18:23).

### 3. Attitude Sins (5:20b–21a)

Eight such sins of temperament are listed. *Hatred (echthrai)* contains personal animosities. It is a firm dislike of people rather than things. The word *enemy (echthros)* stems from this noun (Rom. 12:20). It is a type of anger that wishes its object to be dead. In that sense, it is comparable to mental murder (Matt. 5:21–22).

*Variance (ereis)* is marked by rivalry and discord. It means more than just a difference of opinion; it connotes quarrels or wranglings. Written as "debate" (Rom. 1:29), it characterized those who rejected the truth of divine creation and also false teachers (I Tim. 6:4).

*Emulations* are selfish jealousies. The word *zeal (zēloi)* is the transliteration of the Greek term. Although godly jealousy is good (4:17–18), this was a jealousy over sinful objects with sinful motivations.

*Wrath* is white-hot anger. It involves the explosion of stirred up emotions. It is uncontrolled rage expressed through outbursts of temper.

*Strife (eritheiai)* expresses the attitude of party spirit. It results in "confusion and every evil work" (James 3:16). It manifests a wisdom that is "earthly, sensual, devilish" (James 3:15). It is trying to get ahead at the expense of others (Phil. 2:3) and is the opposite of unity.

*Seditions* comes from a term which means to split into two

[7]See I Cor. 6:9 where it is listed between fornication and adultery.

(*dichostasiai*). It refers to conduct or language used to incite rebellion against authority.

*Heresies* is merely the transliteration of the Greek *haireseis*. There can be moral and doctrinal heresies. They are opinions that differ from established beliefs and often cause controversial conflicts.

*Envyings (phonoi)* express feelings of ill will caused by wrongly desiring to have something that belongs to another.

### 4. Social Sins (5:21a)

Three are given. *Murder*, of course, is the premeditated killing of another. It violates the sixth commandment (Exod. 20:13). It is substantially different from manslaughter or capital punishment (Exod. 21:12–13).

*Drunkenness* includes both private and public intoxication with alcoholic drink (Luke 21:34; Rom. 13:13).

*Revellings* refer to drunken, sexual parties or orgies. They became an integral part of the festivals to the pagan gods.

The comprehensive phrase ("and such like") shows that many more sins marked the unregenerate lifestyle (cf. Mark 7:21–22; Rom. 1:29–31; I Tim. 1:9–10; II Tim. 3:2–5). This list of seventeen is representative, not exhaustive.

### 5. Judgment for These Works (5:21b)

When Paul originally preached in Galatia, he warned against the practice of such sins ("as I have also told you in time past"). This statement, easily confirmed, refuted the accusation by the Judaizers that the apostles' teaching of grace encouraged the license to sin. He always besought them to act like saints (Eph. 5:3). Now, through the letter, he was reminding them again ("of the which I tell you before").

He strongly warned "that they which do such things shall not inherit the kingdom of God." The verb "do" (*prassontes*) emphasizes a life of habitual practice.[8] Such lifestyles manifest the fact that these people have never been saved (cf. Eph. 5:4–5; I John 3:6, 8, 10).[9]

---

[8]The articular participle is present active.

[9]R. Alan Cole, *The Epistle of Paul to the Galatians*, p. 164.

Although Christians can commit such sins if they are not walking in the Spirit, they can never adopt them as their permanent pattern of behavior (Rom. 13:13; II Cor. 12:21).

## B. The Fruit of the Spirit (5:22–23)

The connective "but" (de) shows the contrast between "the works of the flesh" and "the fruit of the Spirit." Works have their source in self, whereas fruit originates from the Spirit. Works manifest what a person does, whereas fruit declares what a man is. Works show conduct, but fruit reveals character. In works the emphasis is on doing, but in fruit the stress is on being.

The word *fruit* is singular, not plural. The Spirit produces *one* fruit, not *nine* fruits. The fruit, however, has nine facets or qualities. If a believer is walking in the Spirit, he will possess all nine of these qualities.

The source of the fruit is the Spirit who produces it in and through the believer. Christ said to His disciples: "I am the vine, ye are the branches: He that abideth in me, and I in him, the same bringeth forth much fruit: for without me ye can do nothing" (John 15:5). The source of fruit-bearing, therefore, is not in the Christian. He is simply the channel through which Christ by the Spirit can produce Himself. The fruit thus is the character of Christ. The Spirit wants the believer to become what Christ is. This was Paul's burden for the Galatians (4:19). To a great degree, it was true of the apostle: "For to me to live is Christ" (Phil. 1:21).

The Stoics claimed that the four cardinal virtues were temperance, prudence, fortitude, and justice. The "fruit of the Spirit," however, has nine aspects. They divide into three major categories with three aspects each.

### 1. Inward Aspects

God is love, therefore He loves (I John 4:8). He loves both the saved and the unsaved (John 3:16). He loves even though He knows that the objects of His love will not reciprocate (Luke

6:32, 35). Likewise the Spirit-controlled believer will manifest the same character and conduct of *love (agapē)*. He will love as Christ loved at the cross (Eph. 5:2, 25). Love for Christ and for other believers will mark him as a real disciple (John 13:34–35; 14:15).

The presence of *joy (chara)* does not mean the absence of trials. Christ "for the joy that was set before him endured the cross, despising the shame" (Heb. 12:2). He did the will of God; therefore it brought him joy. The believer who abides in Christ will also have His total joy (John 15:11). He knows that he can rejoice always because God is in absolute control, working all things "together for good to them that love God (Rom. 8:28).

The *peace* of God rules in the heart of a Spirit-controlled believer (Col. 3:15). In the midst of circumstances which ordinarily cause anxiety, he enjoys that "peace of God which passeth all understanding" (Phil. 4:7). This peace is a legacy of Christ, totally foreign to the experience of the world (John 14:27). It is that inner calmness of emotions and thoughts which rests on the assurance that God is too good to be unkind and too wise to make mistakes. It must be contrasted to the "peace with God" which is the result of a justified position (Rom. 5:1).

### 2. *Outward Aspects*

*Longsuffering* is literally "wrath that is put far away" *(makrothumia)*. One work of the flesh manifests a wrath that is near and inside *(thumoi; 5:20)*, but the Spirit-controlled believer puts distance between himself and this enemy. It enables a Christian to put up with people who try his patience (II Cor. 6:6). It permits him both to forgive and to forbear others in love (Col. 3:13). He does not have a quick temper (a short fuse or a low boiling point).

*Gentleness (chrēstotēs)* is grace in action. It is acts of kindness toward your enemies. God manifests gentleness toward sinners (Rom. 2:4; Eph. 2:7; Titus 3:4). Whereas longsuffering holds back vengeance, gentleness bestows mercy. The former is a negative virtue, whereas the latter is positive.

*Goodness* (*agathōsunē*) reveals the uprightness of soul that hates evil and refrains from doing it. Only God is morally good (Mark 10:18; Rom. 3:12). However, goodness can be created within a believer so that he possesses a spiritual honesty of motive and conduct.

### 3. Upward Aspects

*Faith* believes God. It takes Him at His word. A Spirit-controlled Christian believes that "God is, and that he is a rewarder of them that diligently seek him" (Heb. 11:6). When a person loves God, he will believe His promises (I Cor. 13:7). When a person believes God, he will be faithful to Him (Titus 2:10). The more he knows about God, the more he believes Him (Rom. 10:17).

*Meekness* is not weakness; it is power under control. An ox within a yoke is meek, able to be turned in any direction by the will of its master. It is the opposite of insubordination. Moses, Christ, and Paul were all meek (Num. 12:3; Matt. 11:29; I Cor. 4:21).

*Temperance* does not refer to moderation in drink; rather it is synonymous with self-control (Acts 24:25; II Peter 1:6). It is mature stedfastness, not easily influenced by the world, the flesh, and the devil.

### 4. Summary

Paul concluded: ". . . against such there is no law." The word *such* refers to the ninefold aspect of the fruit of the Spirit. The Old Testament law never prohibited these expressions of the inner self. The law was given to restrain the works of the flesh (I Tim. 1:8–10). The law never said, Thou shalt not love; Thou shalt not be happy; etc. However, the law could not supply the power or the motivation to produce these virtues. They can only become a reality as the believer yields himself completely to the Holy Spirit (Gal. 2:20, 21).

## QUESTIONS FOR DISCUSSION

1. What various means do men use in their attempt to become spiritual? Do they have anything in common?
2. Are Christians more spiritual or more fleshly? What causes both conditions?
3. Are Christians aware of the conflict of the two natures within them? Do they understand how to resolve the conflict?
4. Why do some Christians believe that they no longer possess a sin nature? How can they be corrected?
5. Is the world morally worse today than in the apostolic period? If yes, in what ways? If no, why?
6. How does regular fruit get produced? Compare natural fruit with spiritual fruit.
7. How did Christ manifest the fruit of the Spirit? Cite various events and illustrations.

# 12

# The Marks of Spirituality
## Galatians 5:24 – 6:10

Spiritual character will manifest itself in spiritual conduct. As a man is, so he does. The outward will always mirror the inward. God looks on the heart, but man must look on the outward appearance. Both character and conduct are two sides of the same reality.

This passage is actually an extension of the previous discussion. Note the continued references to the "Spirit" and to the "flesh" (5:24-25; 6:8). In this section, the distinguishing marks of true spirituality will be seen in four major areas.

## I. MORAL RESPONSIBILITY (5:24-26)

A believer who is walking by the Spirit will recognize that he is a morally responsible person, both before God and man. He will be lawful, not lawless; he will always act out of love (5:13).

### A. He Has Crucified the Flesh (5:24)

All believers are constituted as "they that are Christ's" (cf. I Cor. 15:23). This is not a title of a select group of Christians who have obeyed the previous command to walk in the Spirit (5:16).

All believers "have crucified the flesh." Through the baptism in the Holy Spirit, all Christians were identified with

Jesus Christ in His death and resurrection. In Him they died to the penalty and power of sin (Rom. 6:1-5). That is why Paul exclaimed that he had been crucified with Christ (2:20). Elsewhere he added, "Knowing this, that our old man is crucified with him, that the body of sin might be destroyed, that henceforth we should not serve sin" (Rom. 6:6). The verb "crucified" (*estaurōsan*) shows that this event was a past, historical reality in all of their lives.[1] It occurred potentially at the cross, and it was made effective in them at the time of their conversion.

Most believers, however, are ignorant of this truth, therefore they have not appropriated the victory over the lusts of the flesh that Christ secured for them. Necessity forced the apostle to command, "Reckon ye also yourselves to be dead indeed unto sin. . . . Let not sin therefore reign in your mortal body, that ye should obey it in the lusts thereof" (Rom. 6:11-12). Until a person believes to be true what is true, he will try to gain victory by self-effort through legalism. This will result in failure. He cannot change or control the flesh with the law. He must consciously put the flesh to death as Christ did at the cross.

The "flesh" is not a reference to the physical body but rather to the sin principle. This immoral tendency manifests itself through "the affections and lusts." The former probably refers to improper emotional desires whereas the latter points to illicit mental drives.[2] Both stem from the dual physical-psychical constitution of man.

## B. He Walks in the Spirit (5:25)

The condition ("if we live in the Spirit") is assumed to be true.[3] Spiritual life by means of the Spirit was a reality for both the Galatians and Paul (note "we"). All had been convicted by the Spirit (John 16:7-11), regenerated by Him (John 3:5-8), sanctified by Him (II Thess. 2:13), sealed by Him (Eph. 1:13),

---

[1] It is aorist, active indicative.

[2] The Greek shows that they are two distinct categories. Both words appear with their own articles: *tois pathēmasi kai tais epithumiais.*

[3] The usage of *ei* ("if") with the present indicative (*zōmen*).

and indwelt by Him (I Cor. 6:19-20). They were in the Spirit, and He was in them.

Based on that condition of reality, Paul issued a logical exhortation to both his readers and himself: "Let us also walk in the Spirit."[4] The "walk" must be continuous.[5] The two terms translated as "walk" need to be distinguished: *peripateō* (5:16) with *stoicheō* (5:25). The second refers to the standards or regulations which the Spirit uses to guide the believer (Rom. 8:14). When the Galatians were unsaved, they were under the standards or "elements of the world" (*stoicheia*; 4:3). The Judaizers were trying to impose the "weak and beggarly elements" (*stoicheia*) of the law on them (4:9). The child of God, however, needs only to obey the directions of the Spirit in order to have victory over the lusts of the flesh.

## C. He Is a Blessing to the Saints (5:26)

The spiritual Christian desires to build others up rather than to tear them down. On the other hand, the carnal believer is more interested in the exaltation of himself. Paul's exhortation literally reads, "Let us stop becoming vainglorious" (*mē ginōmetha kenodoxoi*). Legalism inevitably places the self at the center of religious activity. The Pharisees, who personified legalism, gave, prayed, and fasted to have the glory of men (Matt. 6:2). The adjective "vain" (*kenos*) means that which is empty or that which has no real substance; thus a "vainglory" may have a beautiful facade but there is no solid basis to it. Believers are charged to do nothing "through strife or vainglory" (Phil. 2:3).

The two participles show the means of obtaining vainglory. *First,* they get it by "provoking one another."[6] A legalist tries to make himself look good by making others look bad. He competes with others on his own terms so that he might win. He challenges others to contests to make them into losers.

---

[4]The emphasis is on the means: "By the Spirit let us also walk." The word *spirit* occurs first.

[5]It is a present hortatory subjunctive (*stoichōmen*).

[6]This provoking is always bad. There is a good type of provoking, but it employs another Greek verb (Heb. 10:24).

*Second,* they reach it by "envying one another." They begrudge others spiritual triumph. When others are praised, they covet it for themselves. They do not rejoice in what God is doing in the lives of others. They are never satisfied with anything less 'than first place. They are thinking of themselves at all times.

## II. BROTHERLY CONCERN (6:1-2)

The direct address ("Brethren") serves as an abrupt transition from selfishness (5:26) to selflessness (6:1-2). The best remedy to negative action is to undertake positive pursuits.

### A. Restore the Sinning Brother (6:1)

#### 1. The Object of Restoration

A sinning brother is a man who is "overtaken in a fault." Why is this issue introduced here? Wiersbe suggests, "Because nothing reveals the wickedness of legalism better than the way the legalists treat those who have sinned."[7] Remember how the scribes and Pharisees wanted the adulterous woman to be stoned to death (John 8:3-5). Later the Jews wanted to kill Paul because they thought that he had taken a Gentile into the temple court of the Israelites (Acts 21:27-29).

The "fault" (*tini paraptōmati*) is an actual trespass against God. All men are dead in such sins and trespasses before they are converted (Eph. 2:1). In essence, it is not a violation of a cultural or denominational code. It connotes a falling aside, a slip, or a lapse.

The man was "overtaken" (*prolēmphthēi*).[8] The nature of this verb hints at the idea that he was not involved in deliberate disobedience. What he did was sin. This fact cannot be denied, but he was influenced by someone else to participate in the fault. In this context, the sinning brother was the Galatian Christian who had been cleverly deceived by the Judaizers

---

[7]Warren W. Wiersbe, *Be Free*, p. 140.
[8]The verb is aorist passive subjunctive.

(1:6; 5:8). In principle it could apply to any situation where a child of God has been led unwittingly into moral and doctrinal error.

### 2. The Means of Restoration

Two qualifications are listed. *First,* they must be "brethren." Family problems should be settled within the family by its own members. Grievances should not be aired to the unsaved world (I Cor. 6:1–8). Solomon said that "a brother is born for adversity" (Prov. 17:17).

*Second,* they must be "spiritual" (*pneumatikoi*). Problems arise when a legalist or a carnal believer tries to correct a sinning brother. Restoration must be done by those who are walking in the Spirit and who are producing the fruit of the Spirit. Only they can act of love and gentleness. Under the control of the Spirit, they will instinctively sense what must be done. The charge is also given to a group ("ye") to minister to an individual. This would involve the minimum of two or three (Matt. 18:16).

### 3. The Meaning of Restoration

Restoration is not a voluntary ministry. It is obligatory for every spiritual brother. The command "restore" (*katartizete*) means that it should be done over and over.[9] It is a continuous process, involving time, patience, and discipleship training. It cannot be accomplished in an instant through a crisis experience.

The word was used by the pagan Greeks for the setting of broken bones. In the New Testament it is the term used for mending of the nets of fishermen (Matt. 4:21). This is an appropriate analogy because every believer is a net, a vessel of service used for the drawing of men to the Savior. If a rip occurs within the net ("the fault"), then the spiritual brother must serve as a seamstress to sew up the weakened Christian. He is assisted in this task by the pastor who was given to the church "for the perfecting [same word] of the saints" in order that the

---

[9]It is a present active imperative.

saints might do the work of the ministry (Eph. 4:12). Through these human means, God is actually perfecting His incomplete child (I Peter 5:10).

To accomplish this restoration, the first step is to pray (I John 5:16). The second is to confront the man with his sin (Matt. 18:15). The third is to produce change:

> Brethren, if any of you do err from the truth, and one convert him: Let him know, that he which converteth the sinner from the error of his way shall save a soul from death, and shall hide a multitude of sins (James 5:19–20).

Restoration means involvement and concern, not indifference. The legalist would let the sinning brother drown in his faults because that failure would make him look that much better.

### 4. The Attitude of Restoration

Two attitudes must prevail at this critical time. *First,* he must restore "in the spirit of meekness." He must especially be characterized by this aspect of the fruit of the Spirit (5:23). He must not manifest judgmental criticism. He must be firm, yet tender, showing compassion for the sinner. He must come as a forgiven sinner seeking to lead another sinner into forgiveness and restoration.

*Second,* he must restore in the spirit of self-protection. He must not be holier-than-thou. The participial phrase ("considering thyself") shows that the person must constantly scrutinize his own life at the time he is ministering to the sinning brother. Paul once warned Timothy to take heed unto himself first (I Tim. 4:16).

The purpose for the self evaluation is seen in the negative clause: " . . . lest thou also be tempted." He must recognize that he is capable of committing the same fault. He must obey the exhortation, "Wherefore let him that thinketh he standeth take heed lest he fall" (I Cor. 10:12). The spiritual Christian recognizes that he will fulfill the lust of the flesh if he stops walking in the Spirit.

## B. Bear the Burdens of Each Other (6:2)

The spiritual Christian will not only be concerned about the problems of others, but he will actively take upon himself their cares. Wiersbe adds, "The legalist is always harder on other people than he is on himself, but the Spirit-led Christian demands more of himself than he does of others that he might be able to help others."[10] He will listen, pray, share, and help in whatever way he can.

Christ bore the diseases of the infirm in that He manifested compassion through His healing of them (Matt. 8:17). He actively relieved them. Later He bore the cross (John 19:17). and subsequently the sins of the world in His body. The believer "fulfills the law of Christ" when he likewise removes weights which would eventually crush others. In the body of Christ "the members should have the same care one for another. And whether one member suffer, all the members suffer with it" (I Cor. 12:25–26). Cain once raised the eternal question: "Am I my brother's keeper?" (Gen. 4:9). The spiritual Christian will immediately respond in the affirmative.

## III. PROPER ATTITUDES (6:3–5)

Solomon advised, "Keep thy heart with all diligence; for out of it are the issues of life" (Prov. 4:23). Attitudes are basically more important than actions because they produce the latter. The attitude determines whether an action is genuine or hypocritical. Three spheres of attitude are now discussed.

## A. Humility (6:3)

A spiritual Christian will have a biblical opinion of himself, but not a high opinion of himself. He knows that he is whatever he is by the grace of God (I Cor. 15:10). He glories in the Lord, not in his flesh, for his spiritual transformation (I Cor. 1:26–31).

On the other hand, the legalist and the carnal Christian will

[10]Wiersbe, *loc. cit.*

180

have high opinions of themselves ("For if a man think himself to be something"). Paul was not impressed by such individuals (2:2, 6). Christ criticized the haughty spirit of the Pharisee who prayed: "God, I thank thee, that I am not as other men are" (Luke 18:11). God hates this proud look and attitude (Prov. 6:17). Someone has said that mud is nothing more than dirt stuck on itself.

Pride is despicable. What makes it worse is when the person has nothing to be proud about ("when he is nothing"). An Arabian proverb says, "If a man knows not, and knows not that he knows not; he is a fool; shun him!" The Laodicean church thought that it was rich and self-sufficient, but Christ declared it to be "wretched, and miserable, and poor, and blind, and naked" (Rev. 3:17).

The result of pride is self-deception ("he deceiveth himself"). This term ("deceivers") is used of the Judaizers who attacked the churches on Crete (Titus 1:10). A person deceives himself when he thinks that he is indispensable, that he is always right, and that he is better than others.

## B. Self-fulfillment (6:4)

### 1. His Work (6:4a)

A spiritual Christian will be concerned about his own responsibility before the Lord. He will "prove his own work." He tests his efforts with these questions: Did he complete the task? Did he do it well? Did he do it for the glory of God?

He is not jealous or critical of another's work. In the parable of the talents there is no indication that the servant who had the two talents was jealous of the one who had five or that he felt superior to the man who had only one (Matt. 25:14–30). His main concern was to utilize the money which the lord had entrusted into his care in a maximum way.

### 2. His Satisfaction (6:4b)

He will take satisfaction in the fact that he has done a good work for God. It is enough to know that God knows what he has done and why he has done it.

He does not wait until someone praises him before he can take pleasure in his accomplishment ("and not in another"). He does not compare his work with others, rejoicing in the fact that he did more or that he did better (II Cor. 10:12). He only measures himself by the will of God for his own life (II Cor. 10:13-15).

## C. Accountability (6:5)

A spiritual Christian will bear the responsibility for his own task. He will not blame others or adverse conditions for his failures.

The connective "for" (*gar*) joins this verse to the preceding one. The reason why a believer cannot rejoice in the failures of others is because he must give an account of himself before Christ (Rom. 14:10). He knows that God will try his work at the judgment seat to determine "what sort it is" (I Cor. 3:13).[11] The words *try* (I Cor. 3:13) and *prove* (6:4) come from the same Greek term (*dokimazō*). Thus God's future examination will manifest whether man's present examination of his work was honest and true.

There is no contradiction in the two concepts of burden bearing (6:2; cf. 6:5). The two words translated as "burden" are different. The burdens of others (*bare*) are heavy weights that need the support of others, whereas one's own burden (*phortion*) refers to a shoulder pack suitable for his own carrying (cf. Gal. 6:5). A spiritual Christian will help others with their problems, but he must shoulder his accountability alone.

## IV. GOOD WORKS (6:6-10)

Believers should be zealous of good works (Titus 2:14). They should maintain them (Titus 3:8). They have been "created in Christ Jesus unto good works, which God hath before ordained that [they] should walk in them" (Eph. 2:10). Works, then, are definite marks of spirituality. Three areas of manifestation are enumerated here.

---

[11]The phrase "him that is taught" (*ho katēchoumenos*) is a present passive participle.

## A. In Supporting Ministers (6:6)

Without exception, a spiritual Christian is one "that is taught in the word." The "word" refers to the Scriptures (II Tim. 4:2; Heb. 4:12). He is constantly being taught, recognizing that there are always others who know more about the written Word than he does.[11] The English word *catechism* comes from this Greek term (*katēcheō*). This instruction, therefore, was formal and precise. It occurred within the local churches of Galatia (cf. I Cor. 14:19).

The phrase ("him that teacheth") doubtless refers to the office of teacher, divinely appointed by Christ (Acts 13:1; I Cor. 12:28; Eph. 4:11). The ministry of teaching has been perpetuated throughout the centuries of church history (II Tim. 2:2).

The verb "communicate" (*koinōneitō*) means to share, to have in common, and to have fellowship. In this passage it refers to the sharing of money. Christians should do this in "distributing [same word] to the necessity of saints" (Rom. 12:13). The Philippians communicated or gave financial contributions to Paul on two separate occasions (Phil. 4:16). It is a fundamental biblical principle that God's ministers should be supported by the monetary gifts of His people (I Cor. 9:7-14; I Tim. 5:17-18). Christ "ordained that they which preach the gospel should live of the gospel" (I Cor. 9:14). Paul charged, "Let the elders that rule well be counted worthy of double honour [remuneration], especially they who labor in the word and doctrine" (I Tim. 5:18). The spiritual Christian will share his "good things" with the teacher of "good things."[12]

## B. In Sowing Righteousness (6:7-9)

### 1. The Problem (6:7a)

The lack of spirituality has two basic faults. *First,* there is self-deception ("Be not deceived"). The command literally

[12]The prepositional phrase ("in all good things") can go with either "communicate" or "teacheth." Both concepts, nevertheless, are true.

reads, "Stop being deceived."[13] The Galatians had permitted themselves to be deceived by the Judaizers many times. Through legalism, they were allowing the flesh to control the source and results of their religious activity.

*Second,* it mocks God. The verb (*muktērizetai*) means to sneer or to turn up one's nose.[14] In legalism, self-sufficiency ignores its need of God. It looks down upon the principle of faith alone as a sign of personal weakness.

### 2. The Principles (6:7b)

This foundational principle of life is clear: " ... for whatsoever a man soweth, that shall he also reap." This analogy from farming can be applied to all areas of life. In this context it can refer to the financial support of ministers (6:6). Elsewhere Paul wrote, "If we have sown unto you spiritual things, is it a great thing if we shall reap your carnal things?" (I Cor. 9:11). The person who sows brotherly concern will also reap reciprocal interest (6:1–5). Sin and righteousness, when sown, will produce their respective results (5:16; 6:8; cf. Job 4:8).

This basic principle has three obvious aspects. *First,* like begets like. Righteousness is not produced by the sowing of sin.

*Second,* the more one sows, the more one reaps. The apostle explained: "He which soweth sparingly shall reap also sparingly; and he which soweth bountifully shall reap also bountifully" (II Cor. 9:6).

*Third,* one reaps more than what he sows. One seed can produce many fruits. Hosea charged that they who have sown the wind will reap the whirlwind (Hosea 8:7). The effects of sin are greater than the sin itself.

### 3. The Products (6:8)

The products are in glaring contrast. *First,* there is "corruption." This refers to the physical decay and moral rottenness that follows the sins of the flesh (5:19–21). The prepositional phrase literally reads "into [*eis*] his flesh." The flesh thus be-

[13]It is a present passive imperative.
[14]The term for "nose" is *muktēr*.

comes the soil into which the personality is planted. Later, "out of the flesh" will come the growth. Sinful human nature can only produce that which is temporal and corruptible. For example, the hoarding of wealth will only produce anxiety, thievery, and waste (Matt. 6:19).

*Second,* there is "life everlasting." It is achieved by planting one's life into the direction of the Holy Spirit. The product out of the Spirit will be a holy and happy life. The eternal Spirit will produce a life of lasting value, both now and forever.

The sowing and reaping cycles actually express those lives which are walking by the Spirit or which are fulfilling the lusts of the flesh (5:16). The products are either the works of the flesh or the fruit of the Spirit (5:19, 22).

### 4. The Promise (6:9)

The conditional promise is preceded by an exhortation: "Let us not be weary." A Christian can become physically and emotionally weary in the work of the Lord, but he should never grow weary of it (Mal. 1:13). The word "weary" (*ekkakōmen*) means to give in to evil. A Christian should never succumb to the pressures of Satan and sin when he is involved "in well doing" (II Cor. 4:1; II Thess. 3:13).

The promise is guaranteed by God: "For in due season we shall reap." A believer does not always see the results of walking in the Spirit immediately. It takes time to produce fruit. It takes years for an apple tree to bear apples, but it only takes hours to manufacture a plastic apple or a car.

There is a time lapse between sowing and reaping. Quite often, believers "faint" before the harvest. This verb (*ekluomenoi*) means to lose heart, to despair, or to quit. Prayer, or total dependence upon God, is the remedy to the urge to faint (Luke 18:1).

### C. In Giving Charity (6:10)

A spiritual Christian will be benevolent and altruistic, not selfish with his money and time. The time of giving is "as we have therefore opportunity." The word *opportunity* (*kairon*) means time, and was translated earlier as "season" (6:9). It would involve both the means of help (money) and the point of contact. Paul knew that the Philippians wanted to support him financially but that they "lacked opportunity" (Phil. 4:10).

The command to do good extends to both the unsaved and the saved ("unto all"). Christ healed both groups. When He fed the multitudes, the unregenerate participated. A believer must always do good even when evil comes his way, both before and after the gracious work (Rom. 12:18-21).

A believer, however, has a priority. He only has so much time and money to give, and there are millions of empty hands pleading for his help. He must help the saved first ("especially unto them who are of the household of faith"). Family obligations precede those to neighbors. In addition, he must care for his personal family. Paul cautioned, "But if any provide not for his own, and especially for those of his own house, he hath denied the faith, and is worse than an infidel" (I Tim. 5:8).

The early church cared for the financial needs of its widows (Acts 6:1-7; I Tim. 5:1-16). Genuine spirituality means "to visit the fatherless and widows in their affliction" (James 1:27). The early church was vitally concerned about the needs of the poor (2:10; cf. Acts 6:1-3; 11:29).

## QUESTIONS FOR DISCUSSION

1. Do Christians understand the principle of crucifixion with Christ? Why do they fail when Christ has gained the victory?
2. Why are Christians competitive? Jealous of each other? What can be done to correct these faulty attitudes?
3. Are Christians afraid to get involved in the lives of other believers? Is it easier to witness to the lost than it is to restore the sinning brother? Why?
4. In what practical ways can believers bear the burdens of others? Are some reluctant to surrender their burdens?
5. Why are men in the ministry poorly supported? What can be done to improve their salaries? How much should they be paid?

6. Do people actually get away with their sin? How do they receive corruption?
7. How much money should be given to worthy charities, like the United Fund or the American Cancer Society? Should churches have a special fund for the poor?

# 13

# The Final Contrast Between Paul and the Judaizers
## Galatians 6:11–18

Throughout his writings, the apostle often contrasted himself with his critics (II Cor. 11:16–33; Phil. 3:1–6). He did not make these comparisons to make himself look better in the eyes of his friends. Rather he was often forced to make personal disclosures about himself to defend his integrity and the truthfulness of his message (II Cor. 12:11). The churches wanted to see some facts so Paul gave them some.

As he brought this epistle to a close, the apostle again wanted the Galatians to compare him with the Judaizers. The difference was as obvious as night and day. In so doing, he wanted the churches to repudiate the false teachers and to accept his apostolic authority once again. Four major contrasts are listed.

## I. IN PERSONAL CONCERN (6:11–12)

Why was Paul interested in the Galatians? Why were the Judaizers? What did each expect to give to the churches? To get from them? Motivation is often difficult to determine, but the apostle tried.

### A. The Concern of Paul (6:11)

The opening words ("ye see") are an exclamatory imperative (*idete*). It can be translated: "Behold!" or "Look!" Paul wanted to turn their attention from what he had written to how he had composed the book. The object of this intensive viewing was the size of the Greek letters used in printing. The phrase ("how large a letter") seems to indicate the length of the book. This epistle, however, is short in comparison with other Pauline literature (e.g. Romans, I Corinthians, and II Corinthians). Actually the Greek terms (*pēlikois grammasin*)[1] should be translated as "what large letters." In the first century both books and personal correspondence were printed with small capital letters, using no marks of punctuation or spaces between words and sentences.[2] In comparison with other epistles the print of the Book of Galatians was abnormally large.

The reason behind the largeness of the print is contained in the main part of the sentence: " . . . I have written unto you with mine own hand." It is possible that Paul wrote the entire epistle by himself, but it is more likely that he composed the conclusion with his own printing style (6:11–18). The verb ("I have written") can refer grammatically to what was written before (1:1—6:10) or to what was about to be put down.[3]

Normally Paul used a secretary or an amanuensis to record his dictation. For example, he used Tertius to compose Romans (Rom. 16:22). The closing salutation of each book, however, was written with his own distinctive print (I Cor. 16:21; Col. 4:18). This was done to put the stamp of authenticity on each book and to prevent the acceptance of forgeries. He affirmed this principle with these words: "The salutation of Paul with mine own hand, which is the token in every epistle: so I write" (II Thess. 3:17).

Since the problem at Galatia was severe, Paul expressed his great personal concern for their spiritual welfare by writing more than he usually did. This fact alone should have impressed the churches. Since he suffered from poor eyesight, the

---

[1]The term *grammasin* is plural.

[2]This is one major reason why transcriptional errors have crept into the copies of the inerrant original manuscripts.

[3]The former sees the verb (*egrapsa*) as a simple aorist whereas the latter views it as an epistolary aorist. The second category contemplates the action from the standpoint of the reader rather than the writer.

largeness of the letters would have been caused by his diffi-
culty in reading small print. The Galatians knew of his eye
malady and were compassionate toward the apostle (4:15).
Thus it hurt Paul to write to them, but he did it because he
loved them. He was willing to suffer in order to minister to
them.

## B. The Concern of the Judaizers (6:12)

Whereas Paul was concerned with others, the false teachers
were only concerned about themselves. This fact revealed itself
in three ways.

### 1. They Want to Impress Others

The Judaizers were interested only in their own appearance
before their peers. They were men-pleasers (1:10). The disposition of their "desire" or will (*thelousin*) was "to make a fair
show in the flesh." The infinitive phrase ("to make a fair show")
is the translation of only one Greek word (*euprosōpēsai*). This
compound word comes from two terms meaning "good" (*eu*) and
"face" (*prosōpon*). The Judaizers literally wanted to put on a
good face before others.

This facade was in the sphere of the "flesh." It was done
according to the standards of man, not of God. In that sense,
the Judaizers were not walking by the Spirit (5:16). Rather
they were sowing to the flesh, and thus they would one day
reap corruption and eternal damnation (6:8).

### 2. They are Dictators

The Judaizers were a bossy bunch. They attempted to impose legalism on the Galatians. They wanted to make converts
to their own cause. Paul said, " . . . they constrain you to be
circumcised." So far, the Galatians had not yet submitted to
the rite (5:3). The verb "constrain" (*anagkazousin*) shows that
the Judaizers were putting constant pressure on the believers.[4]
This was the same verb used to show the pressure that was put

---

[4]It is present active indicative.

upon Titus to be circumcised in Jerusalem (2:3). It was the same verb used in Paul's question to Peter: "Why compellest thou the Gentiles to live as do the Jews?" (2:14). Just as Paul and Titus resisted that legalistic constraint on two past occasions, the apostle wanted the Galatians to do the same.

### 3. They are Afraid of Persecution

The Judaizers claimed to be Christians. They supposedly accepted the deity of Christ and believed in the necessity of His death and resurrection. For these reasons they were accepted into the local churches as genuine brethren. The issue of their salvation and convictions did not surface until the gospel penetrated the pagan Gentile world. At that time they argued that physical circumcision was essential to gain divine justification.

Paul now asserted that the Judaizers took that doctrinal position "lest they should suffer persecution for the cross of Christ." If the Judaizers had disavowed the necessity of circumcision, they would have been ostracized by the Jewish communities. They would have been excommunicated from the synagogues, exploited financially, and probably harmed physically. The Judaizers knew that, thus they were afraid to take a stand for justification by faith alone. They were more closely identified with the Pharisees and the priests than they were with the apostles.

## II. IN GLORY (6:13–14)

There is a vast difference between law and grace. The law was a ministration of death, but grace is a ministration of life (II Cor. 3:7). The law had glory in that it revealed the holiness of God, but grace is more glorious because it imparts His love and mercy (II Cor. 3:7–11). Through the law men glory in themselves, but in grace they glory in God.

### A. The Glory of the Judaizers (6:13)

#### 1. They Glory in Inconsistency

The Judaizers were blind to their own spiritual dilemma. They claimed that the keeping of the law was necessary to salvation, but they themselves did not keep it. Paul observed, "For neither they themselves who are circumcised keep the law." They charged that the uncircumcised Gentile converts were not saved because they did not obey the law yet they were not obeying the law. They were obviously ignorant of this discrepancy which was so apparent to Paul.

These false teachers fall under the same condemnation that Jesus pronounced upon the Pharisees: "But do not ye after their works: for they say, and do not. For they bind heavy burdens and grievous to be borne, and lay them on men's shoulders; but they themselves will not move them with one of their fingers" (Matt. 23:3–4). In other words, the Judaizers were hypocrites.

### 2. They Glory in Their Converts

In the final analysis, the Judaizers were not concerned about the salvation of the Galatians; rather they wanted one more reason for which they could glory in their religious achievements. Paul observed, "They desire to have you circumcised, that they may glory in your flesh." If they could get the Galatians to submit to the rite, they would be able to rule over the churches. They would boast over their ability to make Jewish proselytes out of Gentiles and to change the results of Paul's ministry. Each convert would become one more argument to convince them and others of the truthfulness of their position. Each convert would become a new evidence of their religious zeal and dedication.

Again the Judaizers fall under the condemnation of the scribes and Pharisees. To them Jesus said:

> ... for ye shut up the kingdom of heaven against men: for ye neither go in yourselves, neither suffer ye them that are entering to go in. ... for ye compass sea and land to make one proselyte, and when he is made, ye make him twofold more the child of hell than yourselves (Matt. 23:13, 15).

The Judaizers would be accountable to God for both themselves and their converts. This is the reason why their error was so serious; it was not an academic issue. The converts of the Judaizers would end up in hell.

## B. The Glory of Paul (6:14)

### 1. In Christ's Cross

The Judaizers gloried in what their converts could do for them, but Paul gloried in what Christ had already done for him. His critics gloried in self, but he gloried in the Savior. They gloried in the flesh, but he gloried in the cross.

Paul prayed that there would never be a time when he transferred his trust from Christ. The opening words ("God forbid") literally mean "May it never come to pass."[5] The Greek idiom that begins this verse places great stress upon Paul ("I").[6] It reads, "As far as I am concerned, may it never come to pass..." The apostle was resolved that no one or nothing would ever sway him away from total dependence on the sufficiency of Christ's gracious provision.

### 2. In His Cross

The cross is not only the place of glory but it is also the place of separation. The cross of Christ was an offense to both the Jew and to the Gentile. It was a place of shame. It was the worst execution that the world could administer to Christ. It manifested a break between the holy Christ and the unholy world system.

Christ challenged His disciples: "If any man will come after me, let him deny himself, and take up his cross, and follow me" (Matt. 16:24). Through regeneration and the baptism in the Holy Spirit, the child of God has been spiritually identified with Christ in His crucifixion (2:20). When he confesses that he is trusting only in the crucified Christ for his salvation, he immediately is placed at odds with the world. In so doing, he makes a clean break with the world. The world had nothing to

[5] *mē genoito.* cf. Rom. 6:2, 15.

[6] The dative pronoun *emoi* is itself emphatic in addition to occurring first in the sentence.

offer to Christ and it has nothing to offer to the dedicated Christian.

Paul confessed that he was dead to the world and that the world was dead to him: " ... by whom the world is crucified unto me, and I unto the world." He gladly bore the offense of the cross just as Christ bore the cross to Calvary. The Judaizers wanted to make a "fair show" in the world, but Paul only wanted to please Christ (1:10).

## III. IN POSITION (6:15-16)

### A. A New Creation (6:15)

Every believer has his standing "in Christ Jesus." In himself he has only condemnation; but in Christ he has found divine acceptance. Throughout the Epistles, Paul emphasized the verities which belong to the child of God because of his spiritual identification with the Savior. In Christ he has been blessed (Eph. 1:3), chosen (Eph. 1:4), accepted (Eph. 1:6), redeemed (Eph. 1:7), forgiven (Eph. 1:7), granted an inheritance (Eph. 1:11), sealed (Eph. 1:13), washed, sanctified, and justified (I Cor. 6:11). The apostle wrote elsewhere, "But of him are ye in Christ Jesus, who of God is made unto us wisdom, and righteousness, and sanctification, and redemption" (I Cor. 1:30). The total benefits of salvation come to the believing sinner only because he is in Christ.

No one therefore should boast about his external racial or religious identity because it does not add to or diminish from his acceptable position. He added: " ... neither circumcision availeth anything, nor uncircumcision." The Judaizers claimed that circumcised Jewish Christians were superior to uncircumcised Gentile saints, but this attitude was absolutely wrong. In the book Paul argued that legalism was a major obstacle to justification and sanctification. From that standpoint the uncircumcised Gentile converts could have argued that they were better off in Christ than their circumcised Jewish brothers, but this outlook was also equally wrong. There is no advantage or disadvantage to either background (I Cor. 7:18-20).

What counts to God is "a new creature" or creation. God through Christ has turned believing Jews and Gentiles into one new man. He has made both into one (Eph. 2:14-18). The human distinctions disappear in Christ (3:28). Paul concluded, "Therefore if any man be in Christ, he is a new creature: old things are passed away; behold all things are become new" (II Cor. 5:17). The position or standing has completely changed from sinner to saint. To God and to the informed Christian this truth is what really matters.

## B. A New Walk (6:16)

"Peace" and "mercy" are available to the justified believer who walks according to the standards of grace. This peace is not that which results from justification by faith (Rom. 5:1), rather it refers to that daily rest which comes from trusting solely in the divine provision for holy living.

The verb "walk" (*stoichēsousi*) was earlier used of walking in the Spirit (5:25). The noun form was translated as "elements" (4:3, 9). The peace and mercy of God were not enjoyed by the Jews who walked according to the elements of Mosaic legalism or by the Gentiles who walked according to the elements of pagan idolatry. In Christian experience men can receive the peace and mercy only by walking in freedom under the control of the Holy Spirit.

The standard for the proper walk is seen in the prepositional phrase ("according to this rule"). The word *rule* (*canoni*) has been typically transliterated as "canon." A canon is a basis of measurement. For example, the biblical canon is composed of sixty-six books, the authoritative basis of faith and practice. In this verse the canon refers to those principles of grace which mark the believer's position in Christ.

There is a distinction between the pronoun "them" and the phrase "the Israel of God." There are three major views of explanation. *First,* if the pronoun refers to converted Gentiles, then the phrase would incorporate the saved Jews of this age. According to Paul, a real Jew "is one inwardly, and circumcision is that of the heart, in the spirit, and not in the letter"

(Rom. 2:29). He later added, "For they are not all Israel, which are of Israel" (Rom. 9:6).

*Second,* some identify "the Israel of God" with the true church, composed of both believing Jews and Gentiles. In other words, the church is the Israel of the New Testament and Israel is the church of the Old Testament. The distinction between the pronoun and the phrase, however, would militate against this view.

*Third,* the pronoun could refer to the church of saved Jews and Gentiles with the phrase pointing to the unsaved nation. As a prayer Paul was asking God to bestow mercy and peace upon his own kindred. He was burdened greatly for his own nation which had rejected the claims of Christ (Rom. 9:1-3; 10:1).

## IV. IN BENEDICTION (6:17-18)

The book ended as abruptly as it began with concluding remarks for both his critics and his friends.

### A. Upon the Critics (6:17)

Paul had one final and convincing argument in the defense of his apostolic integrity. It is introduced by the transitional connectives ("From henceforth"). Usually it is translated as "finally" (Phil. 3:1).

The imperative can literally be read, "Let no one render toils or hardships to me." The emphasis is on the "trouble" or physical and mental anguish (*kopous*).[7] The Judaizers and their converts had bothered him long enough.

If the truth of the epistle had not been sufficient to convince the critics, he offered a final proof. The explanatory connective ("for") gives the reason: ". . . for I bear in my body the marks of the Lord Jesus." He not only bore the doctrinal and moral problems of the church (6:2) but he also bore physical afflictions. The term *marks* is transliterated as "stigma" (*stig-*

---

[7]Occurs first in the sentence.

*mata*). It comes from a verb which means to prick, to stick, or to sting (*stizō*). It was used of the name or stamp that slaves had imprinted upon their bodies as a mark of ownership. Sometimes soldiers were so marked. The term was used in the branding of cattle. In the Middle Ages, mystics, known as stigmatics, claimed to reproduce the nailprints of Christ in their own hands and feet as they meditated upon the crucifixion.

For Paul the *stigmata* were the scars and welts caused by repeated beatings. He wrote, "Of the Jews five times received I forty stripes save one. Thrice was I beaten with rods, once was I stoned" (II Cor. 11:24-25). These marks demonstrated that he was the slave of Christ and that he was not a cowardly pleaser of men. His back had been bloodied many times. On the other hand, the Judaizers had no marks of persecution to show for their convictions.

## B. Upon the Church (Gal. 6:18)

Paul began and ended the epistle with a blessing of grace and peace (1:3). He wanted to be gracious in his stand for grace. He closed with the affectionate address ("Brethren"). In Christ they were members of the family of God even though they had caused him much consternation.

## QUESTIONS FOR DISCUSSION

1. How does the use of a secretary fit in with the doctrine of inspiration? Were the secretaries directed as much by God as the apostles were?
2. In what ways do people try to put on a good religious appearance? How can their facade be stripped away?
3. How do people avoid persecution today? Is lack of persecution a sign that a person is not saved?
4. In what ways do leaders take pride in their converts today? Among the cults? In evangelical circles?
5. Why does religious favoritism exist today? What can be done to improve the situation?

6. Do Christians glory in the cross of Christ today? Are they crucified to the world?

7. Does the wearing of religious jewelry replace the physical marks of Paul? Would persecution be a blessing to the church?

# Selected Bibliography

Cole, R. Alan. *The Epistle of Paul to the Galatians.* Grand Rapids: Wm. B. Eerdmans Publishing Co., 1965.

Harrison, Everett F. "The Epistle to the Galatians," *The Wycliffe Bible Commentary.* Edited by Charles F. Pfeiffer and Everett F. Harrison. Chicago: Moody Press, 1963.

Hendriksen, William. *Galatians.* Grand Rapids: Baker Book House, 1969.

Ironside, H. A. *Messages on Galatians.* Neptune, NJ: Loizeaux Bros., 1941.

Kent, Homer A. *The Freedom of God's Sons.* Winona Lake, IN: BMH Books, 1976.

Lightfoot, J. B. *Saint Paul's Epistle to the Galatians.* Grand Rapids: Zondervan Publishing Corporation, 1957.

Packer, James I. "Galatians," *The Biblical Expositor,* vol. 3. Edited by Carl F. H. Henry. Philadelphia: A. J. Holman Company, 1960.

Ridderbos, Herman N. *The Epistle of Paul to the Churches of Galatia.* Grand Rapids: Wm. B. Eerdmans Publishing Co., 1976.

Robertson, Archibald Thomas. *Word Pictures in the New Testament,* vol. 4. Nashville, TN: Broadman Press, 1931.

Strauss, Lehman. *Devotional Studies in Galatians and Ephesians.* Neptune, NJ: Loizeaux Bros., 1957.

Wiersbe, Warren W. *Be Free.* Wheaton: Victor Books, 1975.